THE *Yoga*
OF
THE *Lord's*
Prayer

SWAMI SHANKARANANDA GIRI

THE *Yoga* OF THE *Lord's Prayer*

SWAMI SHANKARANANDA GIRI

EDITOR: SWAMI NITYANANDA GIRI

DARSHAN

BALTIMORE, MD

THE YOGA OF THE LORD'S PRAYER

Cover photograph: Shambhu (Bill Tipper)
Design: Anna Landewe
Copy Editor: Padma
Managing Editor: Shraddha

AUM

To my fellow devotees at Divine Life Church,

Thank you for inspiring these truths to come forth and for the continued practice of living Life as a prayer. In applying these truths, everyone benefits.

With profound love and gratitude of Soul,

Swami Shankarananda

Contents

The Lord's Prayer

Our Father,

which art in heaven,

hallowed be thy name.

Thy kingdom come, thy will be done

in earth as it is in heaven.

Give us this day our daily bread.

Forgive us our debts

as we forgive our debtors.

And let us not enter into temptation,

but deliver us from evil.

For thine is the kingdom,

and the power, and the glory,

forever.

AMEN

Introduction:
Jesus the Christ, a Yogi

Yoga means both the way and goal of spiritual union or
God-realization. The philosophy of yoga is based on the
realization and revelations of the yogis who engaged in
various spiritual disciplines and discovered the eternal truths
enshrined within themselves. They classified their discoveries
and spiritual disciplines into four categories: the yoga of
action, the yoga of devotion, the yoga of wisdom, and the
yoga of meditation. Having discovered the ultimate Reality,
the yogis instructed their disciples in the art and science
of yoga, so that they too could attain the realization of
Brahman, God, the supreme Reality.

The word "yoga" is derived from the Sanskrit root "yuj,"
meaning to join or to unite. Our English word "to yoke"
is related to the same root. The yogi can readily cognize the
yoga of which Jesus speaks: "Take my yoke upon you, and
learn of me; for I am meek and lowly in heart: and ye shall
find rest unto your souls. For my yoke is easy, and my
burden is light." [1]

The word "yoga" encompasses many ideas and practices; however, in its spiritual context, yoga refers to the spiritual transformation attained through the practice of special spiritual disciplines. Yoga is the directing of all thoughts, desires, and activities toward the chosen Deity, or God, Brahman, the ultimate Reality. Yoga is merging individual self-consciousness in God-consciousness; it is absorption in the Infinite; it is unfolding the divinity that is already within you. The practice of yoga guides you to the attainment of Self-liberation and spiritual perfection.

There are four main branches or aspects of yoga, referring to the fourfold nature of a human being: Karma yoga, the path of selfless action; Bhakti yoga, the path of pure devotion; Jnana yoga, the path of wisdom; and Raja yoga, the path of meditation. The practice of these with body, mind, heart, and pure consciousness leads to Self-liberation or God-realization, the divine union wherein we attain freedom from the bondage of birth and death, as well as liberation from all concepts of finitude and the consciousness of duality. Living in God, we expand from the finite into the Infinite, we perceive the One in the play of the many, as well as the existence of the many in the One.

Consider how spiritual one must be to be known as a yogi. What are a yogi's characteristics? How does a yogi live, think, speak, and act? The yogi is serene and undisturbed amidst all the undulations of life—its pleasures and pains, joys and sorrows, births and deaths, meetings and partings, its praise and blame, victory and defeat, fame and insult. Lord Krishna, the avatar or savior, teaches in the *Bhagavad-Gita*, the scripture of yoga, the science of the Absolute, that the yogi "is completely free from all desires of the finite self, and has attained the peace of the Self by realizing the Self." [2]

Let us be mindful that Krishna does not suggest renunciation of desire itself but only renunciation of desires that limit the expression of our divinity, or supreme Self. When we understand that desire is the gift of God, we realize that true desire does not arise from the consciousness of lack but from the fullness of love that desires to share its superabundance in ever new forms, expanded realizations, and in limitless generosity so that human beings may truly live as God intended—in the consciousness and expression of abundance in all aspects of God's image. Personal desire, however, arises from the sense or consciousness of lack. Yoga teaches us how consciously to merge with the Source and thus experience ever new bliss and a superabundance of God's creative spirit and love.

The yogi has not only renounced selfish desires but also is liberated from the negative emotions and beliefs of the worldly minded and the ignorant. The yogi has uprooted the obstacles to the practice of yoga, such as fear, anger, sensory attachment, hatred, and jealousy. Knowing the world to be transitory, the yogi does not seek permanent happiness from it. Yogis always remember that the whole phenomenal universe is finite, that life is constantly changing and passing away, that all forms appear like waves on the surface of the sea, only to merge again in the sea of Brahman, the infinite, eternal, and changeless One. The God-realized yogi has renounced self-delusion and is at peace, for doubts regarding the Self are dissolved in the realization of the eternal Truth. Such a one abides in the consciousness of Brahman, the supreme Self.

Jesus was a perfect yogi, as his life and actions fully reveal. He is revered as an avatar, or savior. What is an avatar, a savior? One who manifests the highest degree of spiritual unfoldment and Self-perfection on earth. In India, Rama, Krishna, and Buddha are a few of the avatars or saviors who are worshiped by countless millions. These saviors, having realized their oneness with Brahman, returned to earth for the spiritual upliftment and enlightenment of humanity, for the inner awakening of the worldly minded, and for the guidance of the spiritually awakened. The saviors are full of boundless love, compassion, and universal sympathy for all living creatures and beings. By their very presence the earth is hallowed; by their benign glance and spiritual touch a human being's life is completely transformed and spiritualized.

Christ was a perfect Bhakti, Karma, Jnana, and Raja yogi. He loved and served God with his whole being, and he loved all beings as part of himself, indeed, as his very own Self. His was a life of unceasing prayer and meditation, selfless service, wisdom, and self-control. Jesus was an illumined Bhakti yogi. Bhakti is intense devotion to the Ideal, complete identification with God. The Bhakta leads a life of continual surrender to the Self and divine Self-resignation. Bhaktas are guided by the feelings of purity, selflessness, compassion, and forgiveness toward all. Bhaktas embrace in their hearts the whole universe, from the most minute to the most cosmic of manifestations. Their God is the God of all—the God of love, compassion, forgiveness, peace, and universal harmony. Their God is the all-pervading Presence of divine glory and perfection.

Jesus was essentially a Bhakti yogi. He taught us to love God with our whole being and also to love our neighbor as our own Self. Forgiveness, forbearance, universal sympathy, kindliness, and tenderness are the luminous expressions in the life of the Bhakti yogi. Christ taught the path of Bhakti, the attainment of God through unconditional love and devotion, for he perceived our natural tendency to love. Jesus knew that if this inner quality would be directed toward God, it would bring the realization of divine Bliss. It is such a natural approach to spiritual union; it is the way of blessedness and peace.

The Bhakta requires no other means than the offering of all one's love to God, letting all feelings and desires reach out to the beloved One, loving and serving God through all actions and in all beings. The Bhakta loves for the sake of divine love alone, with no other desire or motive, seeking no results, no rewards. A Bhakta seeks but the privilege of loving and serving God, the Beloved, and does so by serving God in all.

The Bhakti yogi receives all the pains of life with mental equanimity. By the power of love, a Bhakta gathers and transforms every pain into spiritual understanding and meets all enmity and hatred with subjective good will and compassionate understanding. The more you strike Bhaktas, the more they will respond with the loving forgiveness of their souls.

Jesus' love was free from all impure motives and desires; therefore, he could see God in all and love all with equal consciousness. Having realized God as Love, he taught humankind: "This is my commandment, That ye love one another, as I have loved you." [3] Krishna speaks of four kinds of men who worship God: "the distressed, the seeker after truth, the seeker for the welfare and happiness of all, and the wise. Among these, the wise is the best, because he constantly lives in the divine consciousness of my Self, and is of unqualified devotion. Indeed, I am supremely dear to the wise, and he is dear to me." [4]

Jesus belongs to the wise who love God with unqualified devotion. He gave to the world the fruits of his experiences and fully demonstrated that the way and goal of love are one and the same. Devotees always return love for hatred, bless their enemies, perform righteous actions, and render loving service even to those who hate them; they pray for the enlightenment of the ignorant and violent, and they ever make their hearts' appeal to the spiritual identity and divine nature in humankind. Jesus exemplifies this devotion perfectly. Even in the moment of crucifixion, he turns to his crucifiers and offers them the love and forgiveness of Soul.

Christ was also a Raja yogi. Patanjali, who codified yoga philosophy, taught yoga as "the control of the thought-waves in the mind." By practice and spiritual renunciation, we may attain complete self-mastery and unconditional freedom. The essential eightfold aspects of yoga are: yama, niyama, asana, pranayama, pratyahara, dharana, dhyana, and samadhi. Yama governs ethical and moral observances such as the practice of nonviolence, truthfulness, nonstealing, continence, and renunciation of greed. Niyama governs such observances as purity of body, mind, and heart; inner contentment amidst all undulations of life; self-restraint; spiritual studies; and devotion to God.

Asanas are specific scientific postures conducive to meditation on the Infinite, as well as the natural control of the body. Then comes pranayama, the harmonious coordination of the flow of energy in the body. This is followed by pratyahara, the ability to withdraw one's attention from the objective world and establish it on an internal subject of meditation. Then comes the practice of dharana, concentration on a particular subject or object, internal or external. Concentration leads to dhyana, meditation, which Patanjali defines as "an unbroken flow of thought toward the object of concentration." [5] Meditation gradually leads to samadhi, divine absorption, and ultimately to the supreme samadhi or the realization of absolute oneness.

In the practice of Raja yoga, we unfold our innate powers and achieve the ability to separate our mind from its identification with the body. At the time of the crucifixion, Jesus revealed this yogic power. People wonder how Christ could pray for his persecutors on the cross, in the midst of intense suffering. In his *Sayings*, Ramakrishna, a beloved saint of India, offers this explanation:

> When the shell of an ordinary green cocoa-nut is pierced through, the nail enters the kernel of the nut, too. But in the case of the dry nut, the kernel becomes separate from the shell, and so when the shell is pierced the kernel is not touched. Jesus was like the dry nut, i.e., His inner soul was separate from His physical shell, and consequently the sufferings of the body did not affect Him. [6]

When we realize our spiritual identity and are one with the Source, we know that we can never be separated from that Source and that our soul, or the spirit of God in us, is beyond suffering. We may use our mind as Jesus did on the cross, momentarily to connect with physical suffering. How else could he have demonstrated his freedom of choice to disconnect from pain by merging his consciousness with the Father, opening a way for suffering human beings to achieve the same state of consciousness? Certainly he demonstrated that suffering is temporary and that the yogi can at will transcend it. Furthermore, having let himself experience human suffering, he could relate fully to those caught in the web of suffering and show them the way out of suffering back to transcendent peace and bliss.

Jesus the Christ was also a Jnana yogi. Jnana yoga is
the path of wisdom, or pure Consciousness. The Jnani
realizes Brahman and speaks of this realization or state of
consciousness as, "I am Brahman, the Absolute Self," "I Am
That I Am," or as Jesus did: "I and my Father are one." Jnana
yogis acknowledge God as the only Reality, all-pervading and
infinite, omniscient, omnipotent, and all-loving; yet beyond
manifestation, the infinite invisible. By the power of spiritual
discrimination, Jnanis continuously perceive the truth, the
real in the midst of change. They remain centered in the
divine Reality, God, the Father, and relate all to the One.
For them there is no duality. God and Soul are one
and identical, though called by different names.

The forms may come and go, but for the Jnani these are
only appearances within maya, the cosmic manifestation.
The Self is beyond all appearances and forms. The Self of a
human being is the God of all. Truth is God. God is Truth.
The divine Reality is pure Consciousness, pure Existence,
and the only creative, sustaining, and transforming spiritual
Power in the universe.

Jnanis remove the veil of ignorance by keeping their
consciousness established on the divine unity underlying
maya, or duality. For the Jnani, maya has two intrinsic
expressions: It veils the true nature of the universe and
humankind; also it projects multiplicity. Christ removes

the veil of ignorance and reveals our spiritual identity and freedom when he says, "I am in my Father, and ye in me, and I in you." [7] In its projecting mode, maya is infinitely inventive and elusive. It manages to hoodwink the ignorant into believing that it is the supplier of all needs and independent of the true Source of multiplicity and fulfillment. So long as we identify with the world of multiplicity, maya, we are subject to intolerable suffering and self-delusion. The Christ in us alone has the power to guide us and help us perceive the all-pervading unity, or Source.

Krishna reminds us that the yogi regains absolute freedom. "He who has attained liberation in the freedom of his transcendental Self, and who has recognized himself as the self-revealing Reality, that Yogi alone, having become one with Brahman, regains absolute freedom." [8] Indeed, the knowledge or realization of Truth reveals spiritual freedom, or the liberty of Soul.

Christ also was an ideal Karma yogi. Through the path of selfless service, we can return to God. The Karma yogi cherishes "no attachment for the fruit of action, neither hankering after nor clinging to any object of creation, ever content in the abiding peace of the Self, though engaged in action, free from longing, untrammeled by possession, self-controlled in body and mind while the senses are engaged in action, content with whatever comes after he has made the right effort, unaffected by the pairs of opposites, free from

envy, serene amidst success and failure." [9] Such a one is a
real Karma yogi.

Christ expressed the consciousness of the Karma yogi
when he said, "The Father which dwells in me, He doeth
the works." [10] Also, when he said, "I can of mine own self
do nothing....The Son doeth whatsoever he seeth the
Father do." [11]

Karma yogis joyfully serve God in all and work without any
selfish motive. They have the power of God behind them to
accomplish all their appointed tasks in life, for they regard
themselves as God's instrument or vessel, through whom God
manifests Itself for the welfare and joy of all. Christ brought
spiritual healing to the sick, hope to the despairing, peace to
the sorrowful, understanding to the ignorant, and liberation
to the awakened. He served God magnificently in all.

Jesus washed the feet of his disciples to remind them of the
ideal of true action and pure, selfless service: "If I then, your
Lord and Master, have washed your feet; ye also ought to
wash one another's feet." [12] We are not here to expect anyone
to serve us but to render service to God in all, regarding it as
a privilege and opportunity to experience God's grace even
more fully as God's instruments.

Jesus taught us the highest principles in life and righteous
conduct without seeking any recognition or reward, but
acting solely out of divine love and universal sympathy for all

beings. Karma yogis engage in no action without first offering it to God, and leaving the results as well to God. Ever their thought and prayer is, "Thy will, not mine, be done, O Lord." They dedicate their actions, both mental and physical, to God by remembering that God alone is the doer and gives the means to accomplish all tasks. "Being absorbed in the love of God perform thine action, and ever remembering that both success and failure are ultimate good, be thou undisturbed." [13]

Karma yogis approach all action and experiences in this spirit of selflessness. Thus through every action, they draw closer to the divine Reality and finally transcend all finite actions in the state of God-consciousness, absolute perfection, and unconditional blissfulness.

Thus, it can be understood that these four expressions of yoga, when fully practiced, culminate in God-realization. The Lord's Prayer is a perfect prayer that embodies the principles of the fourfold yoga and provides the means to lead the devotee, or yogi, to the crown of Self-realization.

AUM TAT SAT

Our Father, Which Art in Heaven, Hallowed Be Thy Name

Meditation

Why study the Lord's Prayer in the light of yoga? What can yoga philosophy contribute to the understanding of this prayer? The approach of yoga is mystical, subjective, and universal. The Lord's Prayer is universal because it offers spiritual sustenance to all, regardless of religious background. It is the prayer of our own being, the prayer of every soul. It is completely nonsectarian; therefore it brings great spiritual benefit when offered by any sincere devotee.

The Lord's Prayer is the prayer of a mystic, because only a human being of God-realization could have offered so perfect, so complete a prayer. The purpose of this prayer is to show us how to live in the consciousness of God, how to come to that state of Self-awareness wherein we fully realize God's presence and blessings. The more we learn to offer the Lord's Prayer constantly, the more will we feel the need to offer it unceasingly.

The transforming power of this prayer is revealed to us only through subjective understanding. When we offer the Lord's Prayer, we have to meditate on each word reflectively and patiently, repeating it until we enter into the spirit of the word. Let us become immersed in the consciousness of this prayer, that we may know the consciousness that was in Jesus when he gave the Lord's Prayer. The ideal of yoga itself is expressed there. The Lord's Prayer also shows the way to attain that ideal, which is the realization of God.

Jesus expressed the essence of yoga philosophy when he taught that we must love God with our whole heart, mind, and soul, and our neighbor as ourself. We cannot love our neighbors as Jesus loved, that is, in full spiritual consciousness, unless we first know that we are spiritual beings.

In yoga, we want to know first: Who, or what, is our true Self? The more we understand our Self, the better we will comprehend the spiritual nature of the universe. Yoga begins with this principle: First, know your Self. You already know about yourself—your body, your senses, your work, your activities, your family. That is objective knowledge, which has no permanence. When someone asks, "Who are you?," usually your first response is to give your name. But you have not told me who you really are when you state your name.

Who am I then? If you pursue that question introspectively and with determination, you will find the question answers itself: I AM. The answer has to be, I AM. There is an ancient prayer of God-realization, dating back to Vedic times, which begins, "I am God, naught else but God." The sage who revealed this prayer in India thousands of years ago is unknown, but this much is certain: It was given by one who realized the divine Self of every human being: I AM. This affirmation—"I am God, naught else but God"—represents the highest ideal. This ideal we try to assimilate and live; we seek to enthrone it in our consciousness until we truly realize that we are not this body filled with limitations. We are not this finite intellect filled with anxieties and fears, with problems, conflicts, and confusions. We are none of these. The proof that we are not body, mind, intellect, or ego is very simple: These are all appearances that change. Whatever changes is not our true nature. Only the changeless constitutes our real nature: I AM.

Thousands of years after the Prayer of God-realization was given in India, the Prophet Moses asked God, "Who shall I say you are? How shall I answer your children, the children of God?" The answer came, "Tell them it is the I AM." The profound truth revealed to Moses regarding the nature of God was that God is the I AM. God is the I AM within you. Therefore, I AM THAT I AM. [1] All the prophets, the saints, the messengers of truth of all ages and faiths, have revealed to us that there is an inner reality which will never pass away. It is indestructible: It is the I AM.

You are never anything other than the I AM, a state of Self-awareness. Can you say about yourself, I am not? Can you believe that there is ever a time that you are not? Even the moment you say, I am not, you already have established that you are, because there has to be a Self-aware being to make this denial. It's a paradox, but in the truest sense, you cannot deny the I AM consciousness because there has to be an intelligent presence to deny the very thing you are denying. And you are that presence, your consciousness is that witnessing intelligence.

When you say, I AM, it refers to your true nature, the life that is you. You can never say, I am dead. Well, you may say it, but it's not true. Because who has the consciousness of death? You may say, I am going to die. Even then, what specifically do we mean? We are referring only to the body. To die is merely to lose consciousness of the body. We can just as well say that sleep is a daily dying, because in sleep we are not conscious of the body. As far as we are concerned, the body is no longer there. We are dead to the body, or more correctly, the body is dead to us. Yet YOU ARE, Life IS, that I AM always IS. Therefore when you say I AM, that is your true nature, your eternal Self.

We can therefore express this truth about ourselves:
I am Consciousness
I am Existence
I am Bliss.
That is the triune nature of God, or our true Self.

However, when we make any statement contrary to the I
AM consciousness, such as, "I am weak," or, "I am helpless,"
or, "I am afraid," then we have seriously confined our
consciousness; then we have lost sight of our true Self.
If I say, "I am weak," at that moment I have turned my back
on God, or the I AM Presence. Jesus refers to this Presence
as: "Before Abraham was, I AM." [2] What is the meaning of
this saying? Since Jesus lived long after Abraham, how could
he say, "Before Abraham was, I AM?" Surely he could not
have been referring to his physical body, because it had
a birth; it manifested at a specific time. The body has no
permanence, because whatever is created is subject to change.
Whatever is born is subject to death—a transformation,
or a transmutation. Whatever appears must also disappear.

But what of the I AM? Can we say it has a beginning or an
end? It's always there, whatever our age or stage of life may
be. There is a continuity of consciousness and of existence.
We may recall a specific incident that happened in childhood.
But who is it that's conscious of having been a child, of having
grown up, of having passed through the various stages of
life? It's the same ageless Self. It was there when you were
a child. It's the same Self that is with you now, and will be

forevermore: the I AM.

Do you realize that anything added to the I AM is a limitation? To say, "I am Jane Smith," or, "I am an American," is only to describe what you appear to be and not the nature of your true Self, or your spiritual Self. For example, when you are asleep or dreaming, are you aware of yourself as Jane Smith or as a member of any religion, race, or nationality? During the dreamless state of sleep, who are you? Is there any consciousness of yourself as a physical entity? If you say, "I am the body," then who are you in deep sleep when there is no consciousness of the body? Yet there is consciousness, because when you awaken you say, "I enjoyed a sound sleep, I don't remember dreaming at all."

This continuity of consciousness expresses a very important truth about you. You are consciousness. You are never without consciousness. You may become unconscious of the outer world, if you have a fainting spell for instance; but you are never without consciousness. That inner consciousness is eternal. It is the I AM. Before Abraham was, I AM really means that before anything appeared in a physical sense, before there was any manifestation of form, there was the I AM, or God. Abraham represents not only humankind, but also all of manifestation, the creation itself. Before creation, there is God.

What is God? God is Consciousness-Existence-Bliss Absolute. Therefore, God is not something human beings

have created. The I AM is not created or acquired. The I AM
in you, the consciousness, the life in you, has always existed,
long before there was manifestation. You are consciousness,
and you are life. That is what you are to remember when you
hear this statement, "Before Abraham was, I AM." Before
anything came into being, you were—not as a body, not as a
limited human being, but one with God, or the I AM.

Krishna, a savior from India, teaches the same truth in the
Bhagavad-Gita, the best known scripture of India: "I am the
indwelling Self of all beings." ³ The I AM, or God, is the
Self in us. This has been the realization of all the enlightened
ones. It cannot be otherwise, because there is only one God.
It is true that we have given many names to God, and around
these names we have created many religions, cults, and
denominations. But that does not alter the oneness of God,
nor can any religion change the nature of God. God,
or Truth, is the same yesterday, today, and forevermore.
It is only our individual understanding of God, or Truth,
that changes, but never the Truth itself.

The study of yoga reveals to us that all religions are
essentially one. The differences are secondary; they must
never become primary in our life or they will create conflict
and a sense of separation. The very instant we establish
our consciousness on the essential unity of all religions, we
will have true freedom, joy, and peace. Thousands of years
before Christ, this truth was already recognized by the Vedic
sages who taught that "Truth is One; men call it by various

names." [4] Moses expressed the same truth, that the Lord our God is one God. Jesus restated the same principle regarding the oneness of all with God by saying, "I and my Father are One. [5] "I," the Self, the Soul of every one of us, is one with God the Father, God the Divine Mother—and is God.

The disciples of Jesus wanted to realize the sublime oneness that he had attained. One day when he returned from solitude, from meditation and prayers, radiating tremendous peace, joy, and love, they wanted to know where he had been. Where did their guru go to find such peace, such understanding, such love? They knew he spent time in prayer, but exactly how did he pray?

Then after the disciples were seated at the feet of their master, he taught them the eternal truths known as the Sermon on the Mount. With great longing and devotion they asked their beloved guru, their master, "Teach us to pray."

In response to his disciples' sincere desire, Jesus taught them the Lord's Prayer. He begins with the words, "After this manner therefore pray ye." [6] This introduction provides an important lesson in itself, because to achieve any objective there has to be a means, or a way by which we can reach the fulfillment of our ideal. There is a way to pray, but we have to seek it out, that it may be shown to us.

The story of the disciples asking their master for guidance

also has a subjective interpretation. When a devotee turns to the Master within, the Soul, the Supreme Self seated within the lotus of the heart and revealed within the effulgence of the mind, that devotee will receive the guidance of God. Such a one will hear the voice of Soul, the intuitive message of the Self: After this manner pray ye.

To understand the perfection of the Lord's Prayer, it has to be recognized that this prayer is the quintessence of a life of unceasing prayer. Jesus prayed at all times—that was the secret of his spiritual strength, wisdom, and peace. Prayer was the center of his life, pervading it with great purity, beauty, and compassion.

Even as a young boy, he was established in the life of prayer, or communion with God. At the age of twelve he was seen at the Temple in Jerusalem, praying and discussing philosophy and religion with the priests. Only one who was wholly inspired and guided by God, the indwelling Spirit, could declare with such inner conviction, "Wist ye not that I must be about my Father's work?" [7]

Later Jesus was led by the Spirit of God into the wilderness for forty days and forty nights of prayer. He transcended every temptation by the power of meditation, by keeping his consciousness firmly established on the indwelling Presence, God the loving Father, the Divine Mother.

Jesus prayed each day for "daily bread." He prayed daily for the spiritual healing of body, mind, heart, and soul. He spent many nights in prayer, and during the day he would often withdraw into solitude, into the inner stillness, to receive the Word of God.

In the final hour of agony and transformation, Jesus prayed alone in the Garden of Gethsemane. When Jesus emerged from the Garden, he was prepared to face the world with its cruelty, selfishness, betrayals, and denials of Truth. Now he could face the persecution and ignorance of the world with subjective serenity, for he had reconnected with his realization of his spiritual identity and oneness with the Divine. Always God remains in the midst of his thoughts; God is the polestar of his life. He is completely fearless, for he has experienced the beneficent power of God within him.

Even on the cross, Jesus prayed for the forgiveness of his persecutors. "Father, forgive them; for they know not what they do." [8] They know not, because they are in the state of ignorance—the mental darkness of false beliefs and self-limiting concepts.

With his parting breath Jesus prayed, "Father, into thy hands I commend my spirit." [9] This is the prayer of complete self-surrender; it is the final conquest of all limitations, when the individual self merges with God. Thus it is prayer that leads us from the first spiritual awakening to the inner recognition that God is within us, and that the purpose of life is to serve God, to love God, to live in God, and finally, to be one with God.

Although Jesus gave us a sublime example of a life centered in prayer, nonetheless human beings continue to wonder about the value of prayer and meditation. Some people attempt to pray for a time, but cease praying when they do not gain the results they believe prayer should yield, as though prayer is a contract or special arrangement between humans and God. There is no such God that answers prayers conditioned by personal desires, selfish motives, or impure objectives.

There are still others who do not know how to pray; hence they are deprived of the greatest joy in life. The few who have discovered the secret of prayer realize that it is the way to overcome all self-limitations.

What is your limitation, your temptation, your weakness, your sorrow? Whether it is physical, mental, or spiritual, you can transmute and transcend it through praying aright. Establish your mind on the nature and attributes of God. Whenever any appearance of limitation or lack, sickness or death, stares you in the face, immediately stand fast in your mind. With inner conviction, with spiritual strength, declare, "Get thee behind me Satan....Thou shalt worship the Lord thy God, and Him only shalt thou serve." [10]

Remember that God is with you when you are in the wilderness, tempted by false appearances. You will *feel* the presence of God, the power of God, when your mind is established on God. You will leave behind the wilderness and enter a world filled with the Spirit of God. Guided by the Beloved, you will be prepared to serve and to heal.

To attain the realization of God's presence, we have to spend forty days and nights in the wilderness, symbolically speaking. The forty days and nights represent forty states of self-limitation that have to be transcended. Moses, too, had to surmount these limitations, symbolized in the forty years spent in the wilderness to attain his oneness with God.

Even as Jesus prayed alone in the Garden of Gethsemane, so each one of us must come alone before God. Entering the garden of our own consciousness, we have to leave behind all our attachments and finite relationships; for all that identifies our role in the world binds us to the world. In Gethsemane, even Jesus had to leave behind his disciples, thus symbolically going beyond all the sense faculties and powers. It is indeed difficult to renounce all that is dear to us in this world; for this reason, we experience intense agony before we completely surrender to God. In this self-surrender, however, we attain freedom and peace, and the strength to fulfill God's purpose on earth.

Jesus spoke of the time spent alone in prayer as "entering your closet." When we pray, let us enter our own mental closet. Let us shut the door to the world of the senses for a few minutes every hour, and be receptive to the indwelling Presence, that It may impart to us the wisdom and inspiration needed to fulfill God's purpose in our life.

Let us visualize the light of God within ourselves, for "God is Light." [11] Gradually, we will behold the light, the wisdom of God, operating in all experiences and throughout creation. We will perceive God and God alone, guiding, sustaining, and perfecting God's universe.

Let us be prayerfully thankful for each day's blessing—even the simple blessing of having another day to experience God's grace flowing in our life, appearing as sunlight and rain, as earth and sky and all that is therein. As Jesus did, let us remember to offer gratitude many times throughout the day for God's boundless blessings: "Thank you, Father, thank you, Divine Mother, thank you, Beloved, thank you, Friend."

When we meditate on God, our heart naturally becomes filled with a song of praise and thanksgiving. A thankful heart experiences the peace of God, the joy of Soul, the power of the Holy Spirit. In a life of prayer, it is no longer possible to be lonely, bored, or unhappy. Prayer releases God into our lives; it cleanses the mind, purifies the heart and fills it with love and good will. Because Jesus prayed unceasingly, he experienced the infinite joy of the heavenly Father. He realized his identity with God the Father: "I and my Father are One."

Our Father

Now, therefore, let us expound the wonderful philosophy of

the Lord's Prayer, which begins with the sublime expression, "Our Father." When you approach this prayer from the subjective standpoint, the perspective of yoga, you will find that it has a sublime inner meaning. Have you ever asked yourself, "What is the inner meaning of even the first two words: Our Father?"

The eminent American jurist, Oliver Wendell Holmes, was once asked, "What is your religion? What is your philosophy of life?" He answered that his whole religious philosophy was contained in the first two words of the Lord's Prayer.

When the disciples of Jesus asked him to teach them to pray, he began with the truth regarding "Our Father." He did not approach God saying, *My* Father, but *Our* Father, thus showing that he recognized one common Source.

All of us have one origin: our heavenly Father, our Divine Mother, Infinite Consciousness, Beingness, Bliss. Jesus referred to this one origin as the Father. What does the Father signify? Surely not a god of vengeance, nor a god of punishment, who wants to see us suffer. Jesus refers very often to the loving Father: The Father loves you, the Father loves me. I go to the Father within me. The Father who dwells in me, He does the works. I have come from the Father, and when I leave this world, I return to the Father. I and my Father are one.

Jesus refers to the Father so often that we have come to

associate this concept of God the Father with this particular teacher. But what exactly is the origin of the concept of the Fatherhood of God? We can trace the earliest known references to God as Father back to the most ancient scriptures of India, the Vedas.

Let's start with the English word "Father," which derives from the Latin, "Pater." In Latin it is the Pater Noster, Our Father. The Latin word "Pater" can be traced back to the Greek word "Pitar." And the Greek came directly from the same word in Sanskrit, spelled "Pitar." It is interesting to note that Sanskrit is the most ancient written language still in use.

Thousands of years before Christianity, the ancient Hindus— known as the Indo-Aryans—prayed to Dyaus Pitar. "Pitar" means Father, and "Dyaus" means heaven. They were praying to the Father of heaven.

The supreme god of the ancient Greeks was Jupiter. The name Jupiter is a compound word (Ju-Piter) derived from Zeus-Pitar; the word "Zeus" can be traced back to Dyaus. Thus Jupiter, like Dyaus Pitar, means the God of heaven, or the Father in heaven.

Then how was Jesus influenced by this concept of God the Father? About 200 B.C. there was a tremendous influx of Hellenic thought into Judaism. From about the 7th century B.C. until that time, the people had held the concept of Jehovah as a god who punishes and is capable of vengeance and cruelty, violence and destruction. With the inflow of Hellenic thought, a wonderful philosophy began to emerge. God no longer was an austere, stern, punitive God. Now He became a loving and protective Father. This concept reached culmination in the prayers, in the life, in the realization of Jesus of Nazareth, who was imbued with the religious tradition of his forebears.

Jesus directed us to pray to this loving Father as our Father. When we pray to a God of love rather than a god of vengeance and punishment, we are bound to experience an expansion of consciousness.

Who is the Father in heaven, the heavenly Father?

This Father is not a personality. This Father is the Absolute One, and so this Father is also beyond all human concepts, and certainly beyond gender. But in the language of humans, Jesus chose to call this Absolute One the Father. "I and my Father are one," Jesus said. God is one, the Father is one. No matter what names are attached to God, or what form of worship is followed, or what shape a temple takes in its design, there is only one God. All forms of worship are different avenues to the one supreme Source, the Father, the Divine Mother, the Infinite. All that appears in this world can only have come from the one supreme Source.

Therefore, the Father that Jesus teaches us to call upon is the aspect of God that is the Creator, the creative expression.

The Father in you, the Divine Mother in you, is your creative consciousness. It is your I AM consciousness: the creative power, the providing power, the protecting power in your life. All your creative potencies are manifestations of God, who is the image-maker, or the imagination. Whatever manifests has first to exist in the unmanifested state *as* image in the imagination of the creative spirit, which Jesus calls Father.

The emphasis in Christianity has centered on the Father concept. In Hinduism, God is worshiped as both Father and Mother. Within Christianity, the Roman Catholic Church also recognizes the Motherhood of God. The profound significance of this concept transcends denominationalism in its universality.

We find that Jesus emphasized the Father aspect of God in a society that was shaped and dominated by the male consciousness. To him, God the Father embodied all the noble paternal qualities—wisdom, truth and strength. Jesus also taught and demonstrated the maternal qualities, such as love, compassion, and forgiveness. In his inner life, he recognized God as both Father and Mother. How else could he have prayed, "Forgive us"? The One who is the source of forgiveness must be all-loving, all-compassionate, and all-wise, thus embodying both the maternal and paternal aspects of God's infinite nature. God the Father and Mother is Love.

What takes place in our consciousness when we pray "Our Father" with complete mental attention and full devotion of

Soul? Immediately our consciousness begins to expand from the finite state of awareness to the infinite. God the Father is infinite, God is universal, God is cosmic. This whole creation is the manifestation, or projection, of God the image-maker. God is in creation; God sustains, preserves, and perfects God's creation, all that God has imagined.

In the context of Jesus' teachings, when God is identified as the creator, He is God the Father; when He is identified with His creation, He is called God the Son; and when God is identified as the dynamic Presence in creation, He is known as the Holy Spirit. But all these expressions refer to the one God, the absolute Reality, fulfilling different functions.

The concept of the Trinity was already a part of Hindu thought thousands of years before Christianity. The Hindus called it Trimurti—Brahma, Vishnu, Shiva—God the Father, God the Son, God the Holy Spirit. God the Creator, God the Preserver, God the Perfecter. The three exist in the One, and the One exists in the three. No more mystery. Do you see how simple it is? Yet how much blood has been shed over theological disputes regarding the Trinity!

The Trinity is everywhere. God the Father is life, God the Son is love, God the Holy Spirit is consciousness. Can you be anywhere that is without life, love, or consciousness? Can you find any object in creation that does not possess these three qualities in varying degrees and forms? The

Trinity, like God, is all-pervasive.

All forms are the embodiment, or manifested image, of the triune nature of God, which is life, consciousness, and love. Life is the activity of consciousness. Consciousness is the illumination of life. Love is the unifying principle of life and consciousness.

In understanding the nature of form, we have to understand that life, consciousness, and love are the ultimate Reality. Then the whole universe is the expression of this Reality. Cosmic creation is the effect of the single Cause.

We cannot recognize any object except in relationship to something beyond the object. Form premises formlessness, and image postulates imagination, which like consciousness, life, and love, is invisible, or formless. This triune nature of God cannot be measured in its infinity. We can only measure the effects, which are called mineral form, vegetable form, animal form, and human form. Thus it is the triune nature of the image-maker—life, consciousness, and love— that accounts for the manifestation, differentiation, and individualization of all objects and beings.

The most undifferentiated form of life is found in the mineral kingdom. It shows the least individualization, personality, or development of a sense of ego. Nonetheless, we see the elemental expression of the infinite and invisible life-energy, or prana, in the mineral kingdom. The very fact that the mineral kingdom exists postulates intelligence, which is the operation of consciousness. Intelligence is the conscious activity of consciousness and life. It is responsible for the infinite variety of forms in recurrent patterns of molecular or atomic structures as projected in the imagination of the image-maker.

Among the minerals, a piece of gold, for instance, is a manifestation of life. The nature of gold (or the particularization of life-energy as gold) is an expression of the intelligence of consciousness. The beauty of gold is an expression of the reality of love; and love intrinsically expresses the principle of harmonious cohesion and oneness.

In the plant kingdom, the form is in the seed, as imagined by the Creator. The origin of the seed is life, consciousness, and love, the constituent aspects of the image-maker. How do they manifest in the flower? The flower itself is the living expression of the principle of life. The character of the flower—its appearance and qualities, nature and diversity—is a manifestation of the intelligent activity of consciousness. The very fact that the flower grows according to an internal law of unfoldment or pattern reveals the governing intelligence that determines and directs the development of the flower. What, for example, causes the flower to turn toward the light? Its innate intelligence and desire. What causes the flower to manifest beauty? Its innate love and desire, or its inner nature, which is beauty. It is the very nature of the flower to manifest beauty, which is a visible expression of love.

Why do we feel love for a flower? At first we may think we respond because its physical beauty—its color, texture, form, scent—is appealing. Consciously we are responding to the beauty of the physical appearance, but subconsciously we are responding to the essence behind the form, which is love. We love the flower because we feel the response of love emanating from the flower. There can be no responsiveness unless there is oneness underlying the forms.

In the animal kingdom we also see the operation of life, consciousness, and love. The robin manifests a high degree of creative intelligence. In building its nest, the robin selects only certain materials. It has that degree of innate discrimination to know precisely what materials are necessary for its particular nest and where to find them. What more tangible evidence do we need for recognizing the activity of God's intelligence and imagination?

The mother robin manifests God's love at its level of development when, for example, the mother robin gathers food for her young ones, feeding them before concerning herself with appeasing her own hunger. Is this not an expression of God's loving care?

The love of freedom is inherent in the life of the bird. What more inspiring image can we have than the flight of the bird

soaring upward into the light? This perception arouses our
intuitive remembrance that we, too, have come from the
light. As blessed children of God we have the capacity to
return to the light, or pure consciousness, immortal existence,
and infinite reality of love, which is God.

Why are we endowed with such a high degree of intelligence,
life, and love? Human beings, who are created in the image
of God, have the capacity to unfold to the fullest the innate
consciousness, life, and love that constitute the triune nature
of human and all other forms of life.

It is true that in humankind we see a varying emphasis on
these triune aspects, so that in one person the attributes
of love will be more highly developed than the other two;
in another person the attributes of intelligence or action
may be the more developed. The ideal is the harmonious
unfoldment of all three—the consciousness, life, and love
that are our eternal, immortal, and infinite nature within
the reality of absolute oneness. In the most highly unfolded
beings, we find the fullest expression of love, wisdom, and
life. These enlightened souls include avatars, or saviors,
and sages.

Thus we see that all kingdoms of creation are one, and all
embody the triune nature of God. Life is one, consciousness
is one, love is one. The purpose of all forms of life in their
respective kingdoms is to support, sustain, and help each
other in their growth. And God, the image-maker, is the

Source of all. All these truths are contained in the Fatherhood of God, the Divine Motherhood of God, expressed in the opening words of the Lord's Prayer as "Our Father."

When we meditate on Our Father, we are no longer thinking only of our personal life or personal desires; we are including all beings and creations in the Divine Parenthood of God and family of humankind. Is God not also the Divine Parent of the oceans, as well as grass, trees, birds, stars, sun, and moon, in fact of everything that exists—even the seemingly insignificant pebbles on the seashore, the countless insects, and the worms that crawl on the face of the earth?

Is God not also the God of the mosquito? Some people do not recognize the value or purpose of a mosquito. From the limited human viewpoint, the mosquito is a stinging nuisance. However, from a scientific perspective, the mosquito serves a vital function, because it devours millions of germs in ponds to help keep the ponds sanitary.

Let us remember that every form of life, both animate and inanimate, has a spiritual purpose or it would not exist. It would be spiritual blindness to assert that any form of life has no divine purpose just because we are unaware of it. Inner unfoldment will lead us to understand that everything in creation is an integral part of a spiritual pattern, or whole. In our own life, whatever happens, whether it appears to be good or bad, has a divine purpose, value, and relationship to the totality of life.

Someone once inquired, "When we pray, is it wrong to ask God for anything of a material nature? Or is it wrong to pray for physical help or healing?" How could it be wrong? To say that it is wrong would be to deny the love of God. What is the proof that it is just and proper to ask for these things? Did not Jesus himself pray, Our Father…give us this day our daily bread? Of course, bread has many levels of meaning, but for the moment we may say it is all the sustenance we need for our physical, mental, and spiritual well-being.

No, it is not wrong to pray for help or healing. What is misguided is the selfish prayer, the selfish request, to pray only for what we individually want. If, however, we include everyone in our prayer as Jesus taught— Our Father, give *us*—then immediately we are praying for all beings and all creation. This is practicing Selfishness in the highest sense, meaning offering everything to the Self in all. God is the Self. God is our Father, our Divine Mother, the Creator not only of humanity, but also of every living creature and object in creation. Give *us*, Divine Oneness; don't give health or wealth, happiness or peace just to me, but to all of us. Love thy neighbor as thy Self. Do you realize that our neighbor includes all creation?

When I approach God in prayer, the first thought should be of God, not of my little self or what I want. When Jesus prayed, he did not say, I want health, or I want power, or I want position or family, or anything of this world. Jesus lifted his consciousness to God within him, that is, to his acceptance of oneness with God. In that state of consciousness, when he opened the Lord's Prayer with Our Father, he exemplified the truth that our first thought must be of the creative cause and source of all manifestations. As soon as our consciousness focuses on the presence of God, our thinking expands beyond the confines of our own personal desires to include the well-being of all.

Do you now see how the inner meaning of these two words—Our Father—can universalize our understanding? *Our* reminds us of our conscious connection to all beings; and *Father*, God, expands our thinking to encompass all creations as expressions of the One.

In reading this section, you will surely have become aware of the reference to God as the image-maker. This function of God finds expression in Genesis with regard to the creating of all kingdoms, especially with regard to humankind's origin, namely that God created human beings in God's own image and likeness. This can only be appreciated when one ponders that God is the image-maker, or the imagination, which God shares with us by giving birth to us in God's own imagination. Therefore, what is true of God's nature must be equally true of the nature of human beings, or the extension of the nonphysical or invisible Reality into physical reality as form endowed with the attributes of the image-maker.

True imagination must not be equated with hallucinations or self-deluded thinking. True imagination is the imagination operating in us as our ability to image in consciousness whatever we aspire to realize or create in our life, deliberately and consciously. Thus, for example, were you to desire to travel to another city or country or to create anything that involves manifested form, would you not first see it in your imagination, or imagine realizing your objective before you would physically realize it?

Being impersonal, this law of imagination works also when negatively applied. Thus, if you imagine something terrible happening to you or others, backed by strong feeling, that imaging causes it to become your objective reality. Hence, when you think of God as a loving being, you do not fear God but attract loving experiences in your life and in your relationships with others. When you fear God or anything in this world, by the power of imagination and emotion you experience the consequence of that which you fear. You may know this as the law of sowing and reaping, or karma—action and corresponding result.

Jesus related to God as a God of love rather than as a God of fear. Therefore, Jesus always experienced God's unconditional love. When you know God to be love, the only power, what is there to fear?

Then Jesus guides us to consider heaven.

Which Art in Heaven

What is heaven?

We know what we've been told regarding heaven, but the pursuit of truth reveals that many religious beliefs held by human beings are not based on truth, although they have the sanctity of religious tradition behind them.

No less a master than Jesus said, "Ye shall know the truth, and the truth shall make you free." [12] He never accepted anyone's authority blindly; then why should we? He never claimed that truth could be confined within any church or institution, but he did remind us that each of us finds the truth for ourselves by seeking the kingdom of heaven within. Jesus did direct individual seekers of truth to search the scriptures for ourselves. And he did teach, "Seek and ye shall find." His reassuring promise was, "Ask, and it shall be given you; knock, and it shall be opened unto you." [13] Jesus could make these magnificent promises because he had searched, he had knocked, and the door of truth had opened unto him. He wanted to share with humanity this spiritual law: By seeking diligently within, each one of us can regain our innate spiritual freedom and identity in God.

Jesus implicitly told us where this heaven is to be found. The kingdom of heaven is within us. More specifically, he said "the kingdom of heaven is within *you*," [14] within each one of us. Why do you suppose he expressed it in those explicit words? Within *you*! He emphatically personalized it. Speaking to the disciples, speaking to humankind, to each one of us, he said, God is within you! Where else could God be, since the kingdom of God is within you?

Heaven is not a place beyond this life—and it never has been. Heaven is always within you. Jesus did not say that the kingdom of heaven *may be* within you, nor did he say the kingdom of heaven *will be* within you; but the kingdom of heaven *is* within you, here and now.

Then what is heaven? It is the state of wholeness, or perfection—the perfection of life, perfection of consciousness, perfection of love, perfection of beauty, perfection of wisdom. Heaven is the state of spiritual perfection realized within one's own pure consciousness, even while dwelling in the body-temple.

In the Sermon on the Mount, what central thought unifies the teachings of the master? The quintessence of all the teachings in the Sermon on the Mount is contained in the one commandment that includes all the others: "Be ye therefore perfect, even as your Father which is in heaven is perfect." [15] This commandment reveals the supreme purpose of life. He gave us that promise and personal assurance that all of us can realize our spiritual perfection. He never doubted that we could achieve that perfection. All his teachings consistently guide us on the path of perfection. This recognition of our divine potential fills us with hope and courage.

Indeed, I am destined to realize the perfection of God within me, for God is within me. Where else but within me am I to realize the harmonious state of perfection—the condition of spiritual wholeness and divine bliss? That is your heaven.

We create our own heaven by cultivating loving thoughts, creative thoughts, godly thoughts, and divine love. This spiritual activity opens to us the eternal treasures of heaven and blesses our life with infinite abundance on every level of self-expression.

To find this eternal heaven, we must enter our own consciousness, shutting the door to the sensory world. Only by entering the closet of our own inner consciousness, only by seeking inwardly, can we become aware of the kingdom of God. Heaven is that state of consciousness which transcends all duality, all limitations, all finiteness, and all change. It is this eternal Reality we attain by the spiritual practice of the Lord's Prayer.

Hallowed Be Thy Name

How do you hallow the name of God? What is the name of God? By what name shall we call God? Each religion has a different name for God, and each feels that its name is the correct one. The Hindus call God "Brahman"; the Muslims, "Allah"; the Parsees, "Ahura Mazda"; and the Taoists, the "Tao"; and the Jews, "Yahweh." Since there are so many names for God, how are we to know which of these names to hallow?

As human beings, we all have different names; but we are not those names. Yet there is a name common to all of us. Behind the appearances of name and form, there is a unifying Reality that reveals our true name, which is I AM. Similarly, behind all the names given by human beings to God, there is the one Reality, which transcends all language.

What does a name represent? A name represents, or refers to, the nature of the person or object named. When you call to mind someone's name—the name of your child, of your spouse, of a friend—you can never think of that name apart from the individual. The moment you think of the name, you also have in your mind the image of the person named— that one's character and qualities. For example, you do not think of your child without being reminded of her name; nor does the name of your child come to mind without the awareness of the child's appearance and qualities. When you think of the name of God, what does it bring to your mind? Does it leave a blank? God certainly isn't a blank. Our minds may be, but God isn't.

What is the name, or nature, of God? Infinite existence, infinite consciousness, creative imagination, and infinite bliss, or perfection. The nature of God includes all the noble qualities one can imagine or express in words: beauty, goodness, truth, and compassion. God is love. God is life.

God is spirit. God is light. God is the image-maker. All these aspects refer to the nature of God, the ultimate Reality.

In truth, God Itself is nameless. Even the word "God" is another name for that which is nameless, or the Tao, as Lao-Tzu called it. What we call "God" in any religion simply suggests the nature of God. No one has ever yet been able to define God. All we have ever been able to do is to describe the nature of God. The reason we cannot define God is that the Absolute Reality transcends speech, mind, intellect, and all human comprehension. Therefore we can only speak about the name, or nature, of God.

The nature of God also refers to God's cosmic creation. Does not the whole creation reflect or express the nature of God—God's infinite attributes of power and creativity, abundance and love, God's goodness and mercy, beauty and joy? The origin of all these attributes is the one Reality, the Infinite Invisible called by various names, such as God or Brahman, Ahura Mazda or Allah, Yahweh or Tao.

What is our true nature? In other words, what is our real name? It is I AM. I AM has no shape or form, no dimension, color, or gender; nonetheless I AM is not beyond knowing. I AM is God within us that is all-knowing.

In considering Jesus' statement, "Whatsoever ye shall ask the Father in my name, he will give it [to] you," [16] it becomes evident that he did not refer to himself but to the indwelling

God, or the I AM Presence. Since we know that the name represents one's true nature, then to "ask in the name of Jesus" really means to ask in the nature of Jesus.

What was the nature of Jesus—the real nature, not the personality? The real nature was God...godliness... perfection. Jesus is the personality, or the man who became known as the Christ on attaining the state of God-consciousness, or oneness with God. Thus the Christ, or the Christ-consciousness, is the supreme state of spiritual illumination that each can attain in embodiment. Self-realization is Christ-consciousness. The same state has been referred to by other religions as Krishna-consciousness, Buddhahood, Nirvana, or Samadhi.

Therefore, for anyone to ask in the name of Jesus really means to ask with one's own consciousness raised to that state of illumination exemplified by Jesus. Whether one asks in the name of Jesus or any other avatar such as Buddha, Krishna, or Rama, the spiritual requirement is the same for every devotee.

The name of God has another wonderful mystical meaning. In yoga, we refer to it as a mantram. What is a mantram? A mantram is any word or group of words, such as a prayer, a hymn, a chant, or any other statement of universal truth that lifts individual consciousness into God-consciousness. The true purpose of a mantram is to direct our mind and heart to God.

The purest and most universal mantram is the Word, a synonym for the name. Hallowed be Thy name can also be expressed as, Hallowed be the Word. Since the most ancient times the yogis, who have studied and practiced specific techniques of meditation, have realized that Word. In the *Rig Veda*, the oldest living scripture, is found this truth: "In the beginning was Brahman, with whom was the Word, and verily, Brahman was the Word." Is it not extraordinary that the same revelation is found in the Gospel according to St. John? "In the beginning was the Word, and the Word was with God, and the Word was God." [17]

What is the Word? Countless books and theories have sought to explain the Word, some even claiming that the Word was lost. The Word is not lost, the name has never been lost. It has always existed and will never cease to exist. The eternal Word is AUM.

The name of God has been concealed in the scriptures of humankind. In the many names for God the one Word has been concealed by omitting a letter or transposing the order of letters. For example, the AUM is concealed in I AM. In English we have certain words in which the AUM appears in its contracted form—OM, as in the words omnipotence, omnipresence, and omniscience, all of which reveal the nature, or name, of God. OM is also present in names such as Solomon, Moses, and Mohammad, and in the Buddhist mantram "Om Mani Padme Hum." Thus it is that the name, the Word, which is AUM, is preserved by all religions and scriptures.

The reason that the name appears to be hidden is not that Truth is reserved for the few; but that Truth, being subtle, requires an active seeking on our part before it can be known.

Truth gladly reveals itself to the spiritually awakened, or to the initiated; whereas it appears to be concealed to the spiritually unawakened—but only because they do not have the desire to know, nor have they opened their eyes to see.

Self-discovery, or spiritual awakening, is a joyous experience, which is like opening a Christmas or birthday gift. Usually that gift comes lovingly and beautifully wrapped; but no matter how artistically it is wrapped, you still anticipate with great joy and excitement the discovery of its content. Should you become hypnotized by the wrapping or outer appearance, you would never discover the gift within. Truth, likewise, is concealed under many different wrappings; it is always present, ready to reveal itself to any sincerely awakened devotee.

Now let us consider the meaning of hallowing the name of God. The word "hallow" derives from an Anglo-Saxon word that means to make perfect, to heal. To hallow also means to praise, to bless, to glorify. We truly hallow the name of God when we become absorbed in God and abide in God's presence.

You hallow the name of God by first looking within, by recognizing the nature of God in yourself. Do you recognize the divine qualities within you—the beauty, the goodness and the power of God, and all else that is eternally noble and good within you? You hallow God's name by unfolding your divine nature, by expressing it and sharing it with the whole world.

If you dwell on any self-limitation and think of yourself as weak or sinful, you are not hallowing the name of God; you are not recognizing and praising the divine qualities within you.

You also hallow the name of God by perceiving the nature of God in all creation. If you can salute or hail the Divine in everyone you know, your life will be transformed. For example, if someone is unkind to you, often your first reaction is to return the unkindness. By retaliating, you are forgetting God and allowing your sensory self to dominate. You are not really hallowing the name of God until you identify with the nature of God in everyone. To retaliate is to deny the nature of God, not only in your foe, but in yourself.

You hallow the name of God by always praising God in all things, under all circumstances and appearance of limitations, and by recognizing that "all things work together for good to them that love God." [18] By living in your godly qualities, your divine nature, you truly hallow the name of God.

The instant we lift our vision to the Divine and hallow God's name in all creation, spiritual transformation begins. No longer can we harbor any negative feelings or destructive thoughts when we abide wholeheartedly in the name of God.

The purifying influence of the name has been recognized by all the enlightened devotees of God. For example, Chaitannya, a much revered saint of India who lived in the 15th century, taught the power of the name: "Chant the name of the Lord and His glory unceasingly, that the mirror of the mind may be wiped clean, and quenched that mighty forest fire, worldly lust, raging furiously within." [19] In Proverbs, we read of the power of the name: "The name of the Lord is a strong tower: the righteous runneth into it, and is safe." [20] Jesus was also expressing the power of the name in his teaching. "Whatsoever ye shall ask the Father in my name he will give it [to] you."

Therefore, let us always remember to hallow the name of God by manifesting and sharing our God-given nature and eternal attributes of Soul.

Thy Kingdom Come, Thy Will Be Done in Earth as It Is in Heaven

Meditation

Meditation is the hallowing and unfolding of our true nature, the I AM. It is the conscious realization of the all-pervading Reality, which is ever within.

Meditation has both an objective and a subjective purpose. Objectively, the purpose of meditation is to help us remember to be calm in the midst of all our activities. To be calmly active and actively calm is one of the significant expressions of meditation.

The subjective value of meditation is that it transports our mind beyond the limits of the mind itself. It liberates us from the ego-sense, which is the consciousness of self-limitation.

The action of ego contracts our thinking and our heart.
It shrinks our area of concern to the little self and to what
is comfortable or convenient to the self. Meditation expands
our consciousness beyond the finite self into universality.
It liberates the feeling of our heart into universal love—
the love that transcends all distinctions of class, religion,
and race.

Until we experience this universal love, we cannot feel
complete. Our life will be fragmented until we have learned
to universalize our love. Indeed, love for our immediate
family is blessed. It is within the family that our ability to
love begins and is nurtured. But if we love our family only
for the satisfaction of our own needs or as an extension of
our ego, such love tends to become possessive, domineering,
and filled with anxiety and fear of loss. Only the divine love
that awakens in us the feeling of oneness with all humankind
can lead us to peace and fulfillment.

Meditation is the practice and realization of the union of
the lover and the Beloved. All realization is incomplete until
God completes it. When God is perfectly realized, there
is no longer any distinction between the meditator and God.
God is loved, and God loves. The Self is loved, and the Self
loves. The devotee and the object of devotion merge as
one. This blessed state of divine unity cannot ever be fully
expressed. Nonetheless, we know that it exists, that it is real,
and that we can experience it for ourselves. Such universal
love cannot be known, however, until we feel that intensity

of spiritual yearning in which we willingly and gladly renounce all self-limitations.

Meditation is the specific technique of subjective communion that flowers into the perfect realization of oneness. Subjective meditation is the universal way for each of us to establish our mind on the Universal, as revealed in the lives of avatars and saints. Jesus meditated regularly. He instructed his disciples in meditation and prayer. Most assuredly, Jesus meditated, because without meditation it is not possible to know God. Jesus expressed the highest state of oneness with God in these words: "I and my Father are one."

We delude ourselves into thinking that we can do without meditation, or at least with a minimum, since keeping busy with the demands of the world seems to be the most important concern. To the worldly minded, the world is the most important preoccupation. Where does that leave room for God in our daily appointments? It doesn't.

The worldly minded are completely disinterested in the spiritual life. Even the spiritually awakened often feel dominated by worldly concerns—the demands of livelihood, family interests, and recreational pursuits—which make it difficult for them to discover the beauty and value of meditation. Being dominated by habits of incessant activity and influenced too much by the demands of others, they feel guilty about taking time for meditation.

Even one who practices meditation and realizes its benefits tends to make excuses for occasionally failing to meditate. We may be under undue pressures, emotional strain, family tensions, or the egotistic compulsion to keep busy with the activities of the world. Also our society imposes a sense of guilt on those who seek to have any interior life, because our culture does not necessarily recognize the individual's need for inner sustenance nourished in solitude.

Even when you want to meditate, your family may regard this time apart as an act of selfishness or a threat to the accepted family image and agenda, which do not allow for deviation from the established order. We need to remember the wisdom of Jesus in this respect, that our true family extends far beyond the immediate family circle. "Who is my mother? and who are my brethren?…whosoever shall do the will of my Father which is in heaven, the same is my brother, and sister, and mother." [1]

What accounts for the spiritual effectiveness of the life of Jesus? It was his communion with God, his time of solitude and meditation, his periods of total withdrawal from the world and its concerns. Jesus knew the difficulties of living in this world. He realized that the only way we can function harmoniously, joyously, and peacefully is to remain centered in the presence of God, or the Source within us. From this daily contact and communion with one's inner Self emerge the wisdom, the guidance, and all the means for the accomplishment of one's tasks in the world. Seeking first the kingdom of God, or God-consciousness within us, reveals whatever is necessary for our life and well-being.

Through meditation we reach that state of consciousness where we actually feel all of humankind to be part of ourself—not only the members of humanity that appeal to us, but also all those who are judged to be socially unacceptable. St. Francis, for example, embraced the outcasts of society with the love of Soul, which grew out of his own compassionate understanding. When St. Francis saw the leper, he was violently repulsed because of the ancient stigma and horror attached to leprosy, a condition regarded as contagious. But after his spiritual awakening, St. Francis was able to see beyond the leper's physical deformity. He was able to behold a child of God, who was therefore his own spiritual brother. Francis ran out to welcome the leper, whom he embraced in recognition of their spiritual oneness and said to him, "Not only art thou my brother, but thou art a part of myself."

Mahatma Gandhi, the father of modern India, cleansed the wounds of the lepers whom everyone shunned and feared. Gandhi actually nursed these outcasts with his own hands. What inspired Gandhi to serve the lepers? It was his overwhelming love for all of God's children that enabled him to transcend all human aversions and social stigmas. He saw only the one Self in all.

Gandhi, like Jesus, realized the power of oneness, which is

released through love, truth, and forgiveness. We should be familiar with the life of Gandhi, because in India he is regarded as a mahatma, which means Great Soul, because of his spiritual attainment and service to God in humanity.

A supreme example of his loving forgiveness occurred the night Gandhi was assassinated. Gandhi was on his way to a prayer meeting when a young revolutionary forced his way through the crowd, confronted Gandhi with a gun in his hand, and fired three shots. Gandhi looked forgivingly at his assassin and folded his hands in the gesture of pronam, the holy greeting, which means, "In my Soul I bow to your Soul, in the realization of Soul's oneness with God." Thrice the Mahatma repeated "Eh Ram," a favorite mantram, and he was overheard to say, "I forgive you."

Does not Gandhi's act of forgiveness remind us of the forgiveness of Jesus at the time of his crucifixion when he prayed, "Father, forgive them; for they know not what they do."? [2]

Forgive them—how much there is to be learned from those words! Every day we have to practice forgiveness. If someone has injured us, physically, mentally, or emotionally, we can only forgive the one who has injured us if we have become firmly established in the love of Soul. To love with one's Soul is to respond to the presence of the God of forgiveness in everyone. Unless we recognize this oneness, we can neither forgive another for injustice to us nor can we forgive ourselves for our own shortcomings.

A human being who realizes this joy of Soul invariably expresses that inner joy through a wonderful sense of humor. It could not be otherwise, because the essence of life is Bliss. Therefore to know one's Self is to be blissful. The true nature of the Self is boundless joy, or bliss. Is it not strange that we have no record of any expression of humor in the life of Jesus, since surely he was filled with the bliss of God?

Joy is born of the love of God. Jesus, having realized the fullness of God's love, came to teach us to live in the joy of the God of love. As he himself said, "These things have I spoken unto you, that my joy might remain in you, and that your joy might be full." [3] "My" joy and "your" joy are identical, for this all-sustaining joy has the same source: the God of love.

Gandhi, like Jesus, was so closely identified with God that he lived in the joy of God in the midst of overwhelming trials and difficulties. Gandhi himself once said that without a sense of humor, he would long ago have committed suicide. Gandhi's life reveals many incidents of uplifting and sustaining humor.

For the major part of his life he wore only a simple, white loincloth (dhoti) of homespun cotton as a symbol of his complete identification with the masses of Indians, the poorest of the poor. Gandhi did not dress up for anyone, whatever the occasion. When Gandhi was granted an audience with the King of England, he was asked what he would wear for such a traditionally formal occasion. Surely he would not appear before the King clad only in his dhoti, suggested the interviewer. With his typical smile and twinkle in his eyes, Gandhi retorted, "I think the King will be wearing enough for both of us, so I will go just as I am."

Humor is the saving grace of life. In our individual life, no matter how serious, difficult, or sorrowful our circumstances may appear to be, if we can with determination and persistence detach ourselves from the situation, we can extract some element of humor from every experience. If we have a sense of humor, we can approach any situation in life with a positive attitude and an awareness of God's grace. Humor is the ability to rise above the gravity of any situation.

Why is Gandhi considered a mahatma by millions of people? He awakened the power of Soul in humankind. He changed and uplifted the consciousness of humanity to a higher state of spiritual awareness. He demonstrated that Soul power and ahimsa (universal love and nonviolence) are mightier than the sword, and they alone can free human beings from fear and oppression.

Gandhi's peaceful means, like those of Jesus, were rooted in the recognition that God is Love and Truth, the supreme Power. Hence, only the power of universal love, inherent in the Soul of human beings, can free us from violence, hatred, and oppression.

Both Gandhi and Jesus knew the power of truth. Truth could be realized, and truthfulness could be practiced in every area of life. Gandhi carried this practice into the arena of politics to demonstrate that truth and politics need not be regarded as incompatible or antithetical. In truth, he spiritualized politics. He lived the ideal, and since the God of love and truth is the indwelling Reality in all beings, Gandhi inspired others to respond to that Presence. He always appealed to the noble and spiritual nature of humankind. Thus he hallowed the name, or nature, of God in every being.

Thy Kingdom Come

The Lord's Prayer progresses in a rhythm of unfoldment, so that when we truly hallow the name of God, the ultimate consequence is that God's kingdom will come.

When you pray "Thy kingdom come," what do you expect to happen? In Jesus' time, a large segment of the Hebrew people believed that their Messiah would restore to them the glories of the old kingdom, a political kingdom based on wealth and power. Their Messiah would be of the House of David. Not understanding the true mission of Jesus, they sought to place on his head a worldly crown; but the master reminded them that his kingdom was not of this earth. In fact, the kingdom of God already is established in us. Therefore, our only need is to remember that we can become aware of the eternal presence of God's kingdom, or reality of infinite bliss, grace, love, power, wisdom, beauty, and abundance.

Jesus' purpose was not to restore any political kingdom, but to help us restore to ourselves the realization of the kingdom of God. We already know where this kingdom is to be discovered. Jesus told us very plainly, the kingdom of God is within you. Therefore when we pray, "Thy kingdom come," we are really saying: Let there come into my awareness the realization of Thy kingdom of peace, love, and perfection— which is that state of consciousness known as samadhi, or God-realization.

To let Thy kingdom come also means, *O God, let Thy nature and attributes be unfolded in my life for the mutual good of all beings. O God, let me be an instrument for the expression of Thy grace. Let me show forth Thy perfection!*

Do you know what state of consciousness, what mental attitude is required for this kingdom to manifest in our life? Complete self-surrender. This means we must renounce the desire for worldly power, wealth, and recognition. My only prayer is, "Let the kingdom of eternal treasures be manifested and unfolded through me. Let me be Thy pure channel, Thy perfect instrument, Thy perfect devotee. Unto Thee I offer my body, mind, heart, and soul in unceasing devotion."

Total self-surrender is complete identification, complete union, with our ideal—God, truth, or spiritual perfection. Only by complete self-dedication to God can the nature, or kingdom, of God reveal Itself to us. *O Lord, come! Let It be manifested. O God, use me, use me. Do with me what you will. Let only Thy goodness, Thy grace, Thy love, flow through me, so that nothing finite, nothing negative, nothing selfish can any longer dominate my life, my mind, or my actions. Let me live only for Thee, and Thee alone.*

Thy kingdom come. What a sense of self-assurance and divine trust is evoked by the recognition that the King of this kingdom is always enthroned in the midst of our being. The King is God within the kingdom of each one of us. The name of God the King is inscribed in the forehead of every being.

Thy Will Be Done

What is the will of God? This question deals with one of the most complex subjects in the domain of religion and philosophy.

When we have a happy experience it does not occur to us to ask, "Why is God blessing me, or why am I happy?" In fact, we rather think that we obviously deserve this good fortune without necessarily attributing it to God. However, when misfortune strikes, we blame God, complaining bitterly, and ask accusingly, "Why is God punishing me?" Not understanding, we say with resignation, "It must be God's will." Such thinking is fatalistic and irrational. Why would we ever have the diabolical thought that God could punish anyone or would want anyone to suffer? Since God is all-loving, God is incapable of expressing anything other than love. As Krishna reminds Arjuna, "This faint-heartedness is not worthy of thee. Be a yogi."

If we attribute our misfortunes to the will of God, we do not really understand the will of God. We are simply repeating what we have been taught. But here is the beauty and strength of yoga: It questions old ideas to which we have become attached. Only by boldly questioning and seriously searching within ourselves can the real answers be found. Inner awareness alone can strengthen and sustain us. No theory in this world can comfort our heart, illumine our mind, or enrich our life.

When we reflect on the will of God, the most obvious truth is that the will of God must be divine. God's will is Divine Will. It must be Perfect Will, because God is Perfection. It must be Good Will, because God is Goodness. God's will is Love in action, for God is Love.

Will is the manifesting power of God. Divine Will is embodied in the whole cosmic manifestation of God. Life, intelligence, and love are the eternal expressions of the will of God. They express the nature of God's will.

But what kind of will do we have? What is the relationship of God's will to human will? We know that we are projected in the image of God. "So God created man in his own image, in the image of God created he him...." [4] Therefore, the will of God must be inherent in the very nature of humankind. Yet it is not always easy to know whether we are expressing the will of God.

When people feel justified in injuring or hurting another, they will rationalize their act by believing that they are doing the will of God. Can it possibly be divine will or an expression of God's love to inflict pain on anyone? Buddha, the Compassionate, who had realized the true nature of the supreme will, taught: "No one likes to be hurt, and none welcomes death. Therefore, always considering others as your own self, do not injure anyone and kill none." [5]

Jesus was obviously aware of the distinction between God's will and human will. In the Lord's Prayer he didn't say, "Our will be done," or, "My will be done" in earth as it is in heaven; but "Thy will be done." What a wonderful spiritual insight he conveyed in these words—Thy will!

All too often our prayers to God are selfish desires we want God to fulfill. A holy man, who recognized this human weakness in himself, prayed: "Lord, I pray you not to answer any of my prayers." Among the Sufis, the same thought about prayer is expressed, "Be careful what you pray for, you might get it." When we discover that many of our prayer requests are not really desirable, then we reflect before we pray; like Jesus, we learn to pray only that "Thy will be done"— and no longer mine.

How can we know the difference between Thy will and my will? God's will is free will. So long as we follow our sense-identified desires, we are the victims of enslaved will. If we commit an unrighteous act, claiming it is the will of God, that is enslaved will—which is self-deluded will. Do you know that even God, the immutable Law, cannot alter or violate the principle of divine will? For free will is inherent in the nature of God and is an eternal attribute of God.

To pray "Thy will" is then to bring to conscious remembrance the truth that God's will is a spiritual reality, that God manifests this world by divine will; and that since free will is an expression of God, we, too, are endowed with free will. The Soul of a human, being identical with God, possesses the same manifesting power of will as God.

We know that we have free will, because we have Self-awareness, which gives birth to freedom of choice. We are all conscious of ourselves as individuals, are we not? We can say of ourselves, I AM. No one can say that for us. Only the individual can know: I AM. The very act of knowing is a proof of being, or Self-awareness.

We all have Self-knowledge; and knowing is the activity of consciousness. Thought is subjective action. Every action, whether it be subjective or objective, expresses a choice. We are exercising our freedom of will in every choice we make—and having made a choice, the nature of what is intended, imagined, felt, and desired will be experienced on the physical, mental, or spiritual level. Every thought, desire, and action determines our destiny, now and in all future incarnations. To live is to express free will; to live in perfection is to let the perfect will of God manifest through us.

If we want to find out whether we are doing God's will or following our own stubborn will, let us apply this test: Whenever our will is united with God's will, there must be an expression of our inherent godliness. That is a spiritual law. When our will is one with God's will, we manifest our divine qualities, our creative potencies. The perfect manifestation of the spiritual qualities is an expression of the perfect will of God.

"Thy will" also means divine guidance, because it is only in our surrender to Thy guidance that Thy will can be fulfilled in our lives. Human beings of illumined wisdom know that when we let God guide our lives, life moves in perfect harmony. When we try to surrender to God's guidance, we experience a powerful subjective struggle, a tenacious inner resistance, because we are still seeking to exercise and preserve our self-limiting will. During this struggle, so long as we remember that God gives us the strength to surmount difficulties, we can overcome all obstacles with joy, fearlessness, and self-confidence.

In the measure that we surrender to God's will, we experience God's guidance, which appears in various ways. It is received in meditation, because meditation awakens our intuitive faculty. Intuition, being the revealing faculty of Soul, gives us the direct perception of God's will.

Guidance may come from within, it may come from without. Divine guidance may come through gurus and their teachings, it may come through scripture and inspired writings. It may come through virtuous actions, through expressions of love, or loving service. Spiritual insight may come through nature, it may come through anyone or anything in creation—if we are attuned to inner guidance. Although guidance may come from without, it can only be recognized within our own awareness. By the practice of meditation, we develop the ability to recognize God's guidance in all things and under all circumstances.

When we live in the consciousness that there is only God's will, then everything becomes an expression of God's will, which is perfect will, perfect love. Then we become like the saintly man in this story:

In a small town in India there lived a very humble weaver. He lived alone. His simple needs were met by selling his cloth in the marketplace. He slept under a tree—that was his only home. He was known to all as a man of great saintliness and wisdom.

Opposite the weaver's home under the tree stood the house of a very rich man. One night while the weaver was sound asleep, two thieves passed by him on their way to rob the rich man's house. They broke into the house and filled a large sack with valuables.

When they came out of the house with this loot, they went over to the tree where the weaver was sleeping. Neither one trusted the other to carry the loot, so they aroused the innocent weaver and ordered him to carry the heavy bag for them. The weaver did not know the bag contained stolen goods. He thought they were weary travelers, and he gladly helped them because of his inner love and kindliness.

In the meantime the rich man awakened and discovered the theft. He immediately called the police, who started searching for the robbers. The two thieves fled when they saw a policeman running toward them, leaving behind the weaver with the heavy sack. The policeman, seeing the weaver with the stolen goods, arrested him. The simple weaver didn't realize what had happened until the bag of stolen goods was opened.

The weaver was taken to jail. The next morning there was a court trial. All the villagers gathered to find out what had happened. When they heard that their humble weaver had been arrested for stealing, they said, "How can that be? He has never harmed anyone nor has he ever stolen anything."

At the trial the judge asked him to explain what happened the night before. This was the weaver's answer:

"By the will of God, I went to sleep under the tree. By the will of God, these two thieves came along and asked me to carry their bag. By the will of God, the policeman came along and arrested me. By the will of God, I spent the night in jail. And by the will of God, I am telling you what happened."

The judge smiled to himself, realizing that this humble man could not be a thief. He therefore released the innocent man. And when the weaver stepped outside, his friends asked him, "What happened?"

He repeated his story just as he told it to the judge, and concluded by saying, "And by the will of God, I am free again."

The obvious truth of this story is that when we learn to surrender ourselves to God's guidance with complete trust, inner serenity pervades our life. Human events no longer have any power to disturb that serenity, because we are inwardly free. Such is the blessedness and the power of living the perfect will of God.

Jesus certainly realized the freedom and peace that come through self-surrender. We, too, can have this experience if we remember to call on God's will to be revealed to us before engaging in any activity. Then we need not be anxious about the outcome of our thoughts and actions; we will be at peace.

We need to consider another perspective about God's will as it is specifically mentioned in the Lord's Prayer. The Greek language, from which this was translated, has a tense that was not available in Latin and in the European languages. So, the translation, "Thy will be done in earth," if translated accurately, would be, "Thy will is being done in earth as it is in heaven."

If you say, "Thy will be done," the assumption is that God's will is not being done. If you pray that way, you're praying to keep your will out of it so that divine will can operate. There's an assumption here, born of ego-consciousness, that likes to claim it could interfere with God's will. That's the arrogance born of gross ignorance, to which the ego has attached itself. If we could interfere with God's will, it would mean that God is limited or not infallible. So please understand, God's will is being done whether I like it or not. But then what's there not to like about God's will? It's always for our highest good.

In Earth as It Is in Heaven

What is heaven? When we think of "heaven" we usually have the image of a place within time and space, even as we believe that hell is a place completely opposite to heaven.

In yoga philosophy, however, heaven is not a place, but a subjective state of existence. By our pure thoughts and acts we create our personal heaven each moment, even as by our negative and selfish thoughts and desires we create our own hell. Such is the power of individual thought. Therefore, the concepts of heaven and hell are of our own creation; they exist only in the mental state.

When we are warned that we shall go to hell as a result of unrighteous and selfish actions, it is true in this particular sense: There is a universal and impersonal law operating in the lives of human beings that is known in yoga as the law of karma, in philosophy as the law of cause and effect, and in science as the law of action and reaction.

Whatever I do and think leaves an impression in my consciousness, specifically, in the subconscious aspect of the mind, where the impressions remain as potentials for future manifestation. Those impressions, be they relatively good or bad, determine the nature and quality of my destiny in this world as well as in the next world or plane of existence, and in future incarnations.

The operation of the law of karma can be understood in this way: People who live in a gross sensory state, whatever their station or position in life, will karmically repeat that kind of life in their next incarnation unless they decide to rise out of it. Therefore, whatever concept of life we accept will determine the nature of our life hereafter. In other words, the

individual consciousness of human beings determines
our destiny. We reap the results of our own thoughts and
actions, if not in this life, then in another. For example,
in the astral or etheric plane, your environment will
correspond to your thinking in this plane.

The law of karma can also be defined as the law of attraction.
For instance, in this world we are drawn to specific places
and people for reasons that are not always intellectually
understood but only sensed. However, karmically, it is
explainable by the law of attraction. Our consciousness,
which has preserved all memories and impressions, guides
us to whatever corresponds with our present state of
unfoldment and aspiration.

People of a similar nature will be drawn to each other
because of the law of attraction. This holds true in the case
of both the spiritually minded and the worldly minded. An
unrighteous person is drawn to other unrighteous people; for
this reason a criminal can always recognize other criminals.

Likewise, people on the spiritual path inevitably will meet
kindred spirits. Therefore, they are never lonely even
in a strange city, because God, the real Consciousness,
will intuitively direct them to those who share in their
consciousness. It never fails. This realization is an unending
source of contentment, joy, and inspiration.

The same law of attraction operates in the next world,

the astral plane of existence. We will gravitate toward the community of souls that harmonizes with our own Self-unfoldment. Thus the astral plane will be a state of heaven to the spiritually minded.

There is also a psychological explanation of the way we form our heaven or hell. In psychology we speak of the conscious and the subconscious mind, the objective and the subjective mind. Everything we do, desire, and think with the conscious mind impresses itself on the subconscious mind. Whatever is impressed on the subconscious mind, whether it be negative or positive, is later expressed by the conscious mind. Whatever we think upon continuously grows like a seed planted in the soil of the subconscious. The seed sprouts and becomes visible through our conscious activities. Thus we create our own heaven and hell according to the thought seeds we plant in the mind.

Scripture expresses this law of the relationship between the conscious and the subconscious in this poetic Proverb: "As [a man] thinketh in his heart, so is he." [6] The heart refers to the subconscious, which is the seat of feelings. The subconscious corresponds to the astral or impressional body. The conscious mind functions most fully and actively in the objective waking state, whereas the activity of the subconscious mind dominates in the dream state when the conscious mind is at rest.

Let us remember that within the context of the Lord's

Prayer, Jesus the mystic speaks of the mystical heaven not located within time and space, not perceptible to the mind, not attained by any external means but only through the unfoldment of God-consciousness.

Mystically speaking, heaven is the kingdom of God within us. Heaven is the inner state of pure consciousness, love and joy, peace, freedom, and spiritual perfection—our innate divinity.

Let us reflect on the perfect balance in that statement: "in earth as it is in heaven." These words reveal the profound interrelatedness and inseparable connection between heaven and earth. The one bears witness to the other. There is no need to pray for God's perfection to be manifested in heaven, for this heaven of perfection already exists within us. Why pray for something that is already part of our immortal nature? Our prayer is that we may become aware of the kingdom of perfection even while living in this body on earth.

In the phrase "in earth," the earth is the outer expression of heaven, the inner state of perfection. Earth refers to all manifestations. The whole human being—our body with its sense faculties, including the mind, emotions, and ego—is included in the concept of earth. Therefore, we are praying that the heavenly perfection be expressed through all our feelings, thoughts, and actions. *O Lord, let Thy glory and power, Thy beauty and truth, Thy love and peace, be manifested through my body, my mind, my life.*

Then we may ponder this: What's the difference between heaven and earth? The assumption is that God's will is being done in heaven, but maybe not on earth. What's the premise? Do we believe that God is only in heaven and not on earth? What kind of God do we have then?

If, indeed, the Master prayed that way, it wouldn't make sense. Where is that heaven where God's will is being done? Within consciousness, pure consciousness. In the *Gita*, Krishna promises Arjuna, who is a Kshatriya, a warrior, that if he will fulfill his dharma and fight this battle since it is his duty and training, then his reward will be heaven. Krishna was testing him, of course, because Arjuna was a highly evolved disciple. Most people would have eagerly complied at the thought of being able to go to heaven. Arjuna essentially said, "Well, I'm not interested in heaven. What good will that do? I go there until my good karmas are exhausted, then I have to come back and start all over again on earth. I want more than that, that which is beyond heaven: Self-Realization."

In Self-Realization, pure God-consciousness, God's will always is manifesting because there is no ego-consciousness present to ignore, resist, or deny it. Truly, heaven is the state of harmony, of union, of blissfulness. God's will is very obvious when we are in a state of harmony. When you have harmony you have no resistance to God's will, for you are fully cognizant of the fact that the state of harmony *is* God's will.

Give Us This Day
Our Daily Bread

Meditation

It is a spiritual law that as we give of ourselves, so we
are blessed. Yoga emphasizes this wonderful philosophy:
that we are to give thanks for being able to give to
someone else. Surely we are to be thankful for the things
we receive; but even more our thought should be,
"What can we give of ourselves?" If we expect only
to receive from others, we do not grow; we remain
self-centered. The law of self-unfoldment requires
that we give of ourselves.

What can we give to others? Material goods, of course,
are a part of giving, but material giving comes spontaneously
if our heart is responsive to the needs of others. As we
concentrate on self-giving—the activity of sharing
our inner resources and abilities—we will find many
opportunities and ways to share with others. Thus
we become channels of blessing to the world.

We do not have to culture the thought, "What will I receive?" since self-centered thinking arises quite naturally and without effort. Let us reverse our thinking from the self-centered attitude, "What can I get?" to the expansive thought, "What can I give of myself to another?" Then we are blessed, for it is indeed more blessed to give than to receive. Receive we shall, because that is the law of karma, which operates impersonally in everyone's life. "Whatsoever a man soweth, that shall he also reap." [1] As you give, so shall it be given unto you. "With what measure ye mete, it shall be measured to you again." [2]

Yoga teaches us to expand our mind, our consciousness, our heart, into universal consciousness, or God-consciousness, so that we may be instruments of spiritual effectiveness and service to the world. Yogis pray that God may use us unreservedly. Let each of us pray, *O Lord, use me in any way that You will. Let me go wherever You need me. Let my life be completely dedicated to Your service in Your creation.*

Our human sufferings arise because we hold back from allowing God to use us fully, constantly, and in all situations. We may say, "Yes, Lord, I want to serve You. I want to grow in knowledge and wisdom, that I may live and serve more wisely." But there is always a reservation in our mind that asks, "But what if God should ask me to give up something?" In this internal dialogue, we promise, "I'll do anything for you, God, but this one thing"—and "this one thing" is always some form of attachment that prevents us from knowing and fulfilling God's will. God can only reveal Itself to us to the degree that we surrender ourselves to God's guidance.

The purpose of yoga is the total transformation of our life, so that we perceive God as the underlying unity in all. This is not an abstract perception or an idle dream; this transformation is not only possible but necessary for our spiritual evolution and enlightenment. The enlightened way of living—in fact, the *natural* way from a spiritual point of view—is to perceive the One in the many and the many in the One, to know that all are sustained by the same Source and guided by the same creative Intelligence. When we perceive all of life as God, we feel perfect oneness.

We have to *feel* oneness. This is not merely an intellectual concept or achievement of the mind. If you have ever felt a closeness or at-one-ment with another being or creature, then you have had a glimpse of this oneness. If you can feel it with one, why should it not be possible to feel it with all? In fact, it is inevitable to do so because the nature of Soul is oneness. Our purpose is to *discover* that oneness and to perceive it in the world of duality.

We help generate the feeling of oneness by meeting for meditation, prayer, spiritual study, and mutual supportiveness. When we worship together, we create a vortex of spiritual energy, which goes out to the world as a blessing to all. In this connection, we can better understand the revelation of Jesus when he said, "If I be lifted up…[I] will draw all men unto me." [3] This revelation signifies that as the individual consciousness is raised, it is able to uplift the consciousness of others. This truth is a universal principle readily available to all.

It is vitally important that we have centers of worship for generating spiritual consciousness into the world. Without such spiritual aid, human beings will blindly continue to pursue the path of suffering and self-destruction. We can no longer depend on others to be responsible for the welfare of humankind. We have to be totally and actively committed to the enlightenment of all. The light that is within us must be shared with all if the world is to become free from the darkness of ignorance, superstition, and fear.

Let our homes become centers of God-consciousness. Let there be sharing of spiritual idealism, sacred literature, and times for meditation and prayer. All members of the family should be encouraged to contribute their own genuine insights, so that the whole family may gain a greater appreciation and understanding of God manifesting through each. When we let the light and love of God guide our families, we are all drawn closer to each other in the bond of spiritual oneness and mutual helpfulness. Then our homes become centers of God-consciousness and joyful worship.

Worship itself is the expression of the love of God within us.

There are many different external *forms* of worship practiced by people of all faiths. When people quarrel over the forms and become emotionally carried away by the rituals, they lose touch with the spirit of worship. Yoga emphasizes the spirit and not the form. "God is a Spirit: and they that worship him must worship him in spirit and in truth." [4] All paths are equally good because all lead to God. As Krishna reveals in the *Gita*, "It is my path which men follow, through all avenues of [worship.]" [5] The path to follow is an individual choice based on one's need, temperament, understanding, and state of unfoldment. In the light of Krishna's teaching, it is important to realize that we should be made aware that there are many valid ways to relate to God and attain the identical goal.

In yoga there are as many ways to God as there are human beings. God has enshrined the way to the Divine within each of us, because the way to God is Soul within us. "I am the way," Jesus declared in speaking of God within all human beings. In fact, it is only through Soul, or God within us, that we can realize our spiritual perfection, or oneness with the Father. "No man cometh unto the Father, but by Me." [6] This "me" is the Soul; hence, only by way of Soul can we come to God the Father. All forms of worship therefore have their value to the degree that they help us reach our goal—God-realization. What Jesus refers to as the Father is the source of all life and love—divinity itself, neither male nor female.

Worship begins with meditation, with the thought of God.

When we meditate, we should sit with spine, neck, and head erect, hands placed on the thighs with palms turned upward. The reason for this physical meditative posture is that it keeps the spine comfortably straight without creating any physical discomfort. The act of keeping the palms turned upward represents the spirit of receptivity to the inflow of God's inspiration, guidance, healing, and strength.

The significance of all spiritual practices is illuminated in the light of yoga. Originally, most rituals and ceremonies were an outgrowth of direct spiritual insight. Gradually, however, when we forgot their spiritual significance, rituals became dogmatized. The true yogi, or devotee of God, continues to understand and ponder their spiritual meaning. A yogi's worship is centered in God, not in the observance of external rituals. Meditation is worshiping God in spirit and in truth. Yoga is meditation, and meditation is yoga.

In meditation, let us establish our consciousness at the center of the forehead, just between and above the eyebrows, where we visualize light, the soothing white effulgence. Remember, God is light. Sustained concentration on the inner light gradually frees the mind from all thoughts and images. In learning to meditate, the self-indulgent mind does not want to yield to any self-discipline or self-control. The rebellious mind projects a torrent of sensory thoughts and images in order to maintain its supremacy over the life of the spiritual aspirant. If we struggle to dislodge these diabolical distractions, we create internal conflict and tension.

In some cases, this struggle results in headache.

When you feel tense or distressed about negative or impure thoughts, choose to become an impartial observer of these impressions. Do not resist them, for in resisting them you strengthen their activity and you yourself remain in a state of distraction and your spiritual vitality is depleted. In this internal struggle, fighting undesirable thoughts will exhaust you before you exhaust the thoughts.

When you step back to observe your restless thoughts, you will make an important discovery: There is an internal Witness that stands apart from the mind. In other words, you are not your mind; you are the thinker beyond the mind. The Self, your inner consciousness, is able to observe thoughts because it is the unchanging Witness of the whole world of phenomena, both external and internal.

What does it mean, to observe our thoughts? To observe them means that you do not judge according to appearances; you do not label thoughts as good or bad. The moment you judge thoughts as good or bad, you give power to them. When these thoughts become imprisoned in your mind, you become their prisoners in your experience. If you do not fight these turbulent thoughts, they will gradually fade away, and the mind will become calm.

The mind may be compared to an intensely active child. The more we order a fidgety child to sit down and be still, the more the child will demonstrate restless behavior. But if we let a child play out its restlessness, it will soon tire and be ready to settle down.

When we can calmly and impartially observe our thoughts, we do not create mental tension, inner conflict, or despair for ourselves. By practicing self-observation, we free our mind from false identifications and sensory impressions. Furthermore, in this state of self-observation we experience inner calmness.

In this respect, the sun offers a wonderful analogy. The sun knows that its true nature is to shine. Clouds may darken the face of the sun, but the sun does not resist or fear the clouds. In a figurative sense the sun says, "All right clouds, come on. I'm ready for you." The sun, knowing that its own nature is to reveal light, dissolves anything that is unlike it.

Even so, the light of Soul dissolves the finite thoughts that badger the mind. Meditation allows the light of Soul to shine mightily so that all restless and distracting thoughts eventually melt away. This meditative experience expands our vision into infinite purity.

Give Us This Day Our Daily Bread

When Jesus prays, "Give us this day our daily bread," it appears that he is asking God for something specific or finite.

Before discussing the significance of bread, let us consider the nature of approaching God in the spirit of asking.

It is a spiritual law that to receive from God, we have to come to God in a state of receptivity. We have to desire God so completely that no other desire can any longer distract us. Can we imagine the intense yearning that Jesus felt for God in his prayer? Jesus voices this law of seeking in the words, "Ask, and it shall be given you; seek, and ye shall find; knock, and it shall be opened unto you." [7]

To feel intensely the need for more light, wisdom, and peace is in itself a blessing. Indeed, "Blessed are they which do hunger and thirst...for they shall be filled." [8] When we are physically hungry and thirsty, we seek to satisfy that need by food and drink. Likewise, when we hunger and thirst for God, nothing but partaking of God's nature can fulfill that yearning. To realize God we must *want* and *ask* before we can *receive*.

When we hunger for God, we often want others to feel the same yearning. This in itself is a noble desire, but on the spiritual path each one has to feel this need for oneself. It is both unwise and unrighteous to try to impose our personal desires on anyone else. Even the most worldly minded will eventually awaken to the divine impulse, especially after they realize that the world does not provide the fulfillment of their inmost longings.

The physical law states that water seeks its own level. Even so, the spiritual law reveals that we are attracted to people or places that mirror our own level of unfoldment. We must all be free to seek our own level of expression before we can advance to the next stage of self-unfoldment.

Although we cannot force a change of consciousness on another, we can be instrumental in uplifting another by our own spiritual integrity. Let us be a light unto each other. As Jesus said, "Let your light so shine before men, that they may see your good works, and glorify your Father which is in heaven." [9] If your light shines, your whole countenance will show it forth and bring inspiration and joy to those who are reaching out for light. It is the nature of light to share itself with others.

Personal example is always more effective than any amount of moralizing. Is it any wonder others do not respond to our words if we preach one thing and practice another?

We vibrate our own level of consciousness at all times. As we encounter others, we are knowingly or intuitively aware of these subtle vibrations and we react accordingly. Thus do we affect others by our mental atmosphere, for better or for worse. Those of a similar vibration are naturally responsive to each other, whereas those of a dissimilar vibration tend to react and forcibly repel each other. Thus by first uplifting ourselves or raising our vibration, we can uplift others to a greater degree of God-awareness.

Those of a similar vibration, or state of consciousness, invariably will attract each other according to the law of mutual spiritual attraction. The spiritual consciousness may be compared to a magnet that attracts even those who are not as advanced, to provide them with a center of stability and spiritual strength. The worldly minded, too, feel the pull of others who share their materialistic values.

It is very important for the spiritually minded to seek out the company of the illumined, and not to be in a hurry to enlighten the evil-minded. Until we ourselves gain sufficient spiritual strength, it is not wise to keep company with the evil-minded in the hope of enlightening them, because by associating with them we may be unduly influenced by their negativity and ego-centeredness. As the Buddha taught: "He who associates with the unrighteous and the ignorant suffers from manifold sorrows, like living in constant misery with the enemy. Fellowship with the virtuous is joyous and inspiring, like living with loved ones." [10] Let us first become firmly established in the spiritual life before attempting to guide others on the path.

If you continue to associate with an intensely negative person, one of two things will happen: Either your own spiritual atmosphere will have a beneficent influence on that person, or the other's overpowering negativity will drag you down. Keep company with the virtuous, is the wise instruction of the great sage, Swami Shankarachariya.

When you first plant a tender, young tree, it has to be fenced in to protect it. The same principle applies to the nurturing of your inner life. You have to protect it with a fence of spiritual thoughts, spiritual consciousness, spiritual companionship. When you have grown in spiritual strength, like the tree that has outgrown its fence, you no longer need external protection but will provide protection for those who are less strong.

When we attain spiritual maturity, like Buddha or Jesus, we will be able to help others reach a higher state of spiritual awareness—but only if the others are receptive and responsive to the divine impulse. Jesus could have helped Judas had Judas been spiritually humble and open to Jesus' guidance. When the disciple is ready, the guru's guidance is readily available.

In the Lord's Prayer, Jesus offers humankind the necessary spiritual guidance for which the disciple yearns. Jesus himself felt the need for God's grace when he prayed, "Give *us* this day our daily bread." His prayer is totally unselfish, for it includes the spiritual good of all.

True prayer is free from any selfish motive. It knows no beggary. Our relationship with God is like that of a child to its parent. God joyously provides for the child when the child approaches the Divine with the consciousness that the Divine, out of infinite love, supplies all the child's needs even before the child is aware of any specific needs. "For your heavenly

Father knoweth that ye have need of all these things." [11]
So long as we have a beggar's consciousness, our whole
life will reflect a sense of lack.

It is not necessary to beg God for anything because we are
God's children, and it is the Father's good pleasure to give
us the kingdom. All that the Father has is ours because we
are created in God's nature and endowed with God's
resources. To beg for what God has already given us is as
absurd as to tell the sun to shine.

When we pray, let us *claim* God's blessings, God's healing
power, love, and bounty. "What things soever ye desire,
when ye pray, believe that ye receive them, and ye shall
have them." [12] In the highest sense, prayer means to
acknowledge God's presence and unfailing provisions. By
prayer we make ourselves receptive to God's beneficence.

When Jesus prayed to the Father to give us our daily bread,
he acknowledged God the Father as the source and the
bestower of all good things in life—all that is needed in
order to function in this plane of existence. God is the only
source and cause of all that appears in our life as sustenance.
The objective world, which often appears to be the source,
is only the channel for the flow of God's grace. Jesus knew
no one can exist even for a moment without God's
provision, or daily bread.

We have all prayed to God for the fulfillment of specific

requests, but frequently it appears that such prayers have gone unanswered, because God does not answer selfish requests or demands. There is no such God who caters to our will. With this profound understanding Jesus prayed, "*Thy* will be done."

The consciousness and attitude in praying is of paramount importance, since subjective expectation determines the outcome of prayer. There is a way to ask for our daily bread, and it is simply this: Ask with an open mind and heart, completely trusting in God. Jesus could not have prayed for God to give us our daily bread unless he had absolute and unfailing trust in God's understanding of, and responsiveness to, our true needs.

When we pray "give us," we have to be prepared to receive willingly whatever God chooses for us. This willing acceptance of God's guidance comes only after gradual surrender of one's life to God. When the spirit of self-surrender governs us, then we will regard all our experiences as the grace of God.

Until we realize that God is the supreme Good, we continue to suffer from the delusion that God also sends those things that seem to be negative. Whence come the negative conditions, if not from God? These conditions are the activity of the ego-sense, which always judges according to whether an experience is painful or pleasurable. Since the ego-sense concentrates on the negative aspects of life, its experience is consequently pain-bearing and disappointing. Please remember that whatever comes from God must be ultimately good, since God embodies all that is spiritually Good.

When we accept God's will for us, then we can no longer indulge in any harmful actions. We can only do that which is good, because God can only manifest as Good. And God can only be manifested to the world through those who allow themselves to be used by God as channels of the supreme Good.

The question might arise: Since the omniscient God already knows our needs long before we do, why should we have to pray for our daily bread? We have to pray so that we may know, feel, and experience consciously God's abundance and activity in our life. We have to acknowledge that God can transform our lives, that God can manifest divinity and divine attributes through us. It is our individual subjective state of receptivity that makes possible the flow of God's treasures in full measure. If we do not pray to the Divine for our daily bread, we are not acknowledging the source of all our blessings, and we will look in the world of appearances for daily bread, which will not satisfy.

No one knows from moment to moment what God has in store for each one of us. For this reason, we have to direct our mind and heart to God, claiming and acknowledging God's presence often throughout the day. *O Father-Mother God, give us this day greater illumination, greater awareness,*

*greater understanding. Let us be conscious of your activity
in everything.*

When we pray for God to give us our daily bread, we are
also acknowledging that it is God's joy to fulfill all our true
needs. We know it is God's pleasure to give us divine joy,
because God is Bliss. Since God is Bliss and we are immortal
children of God, it is our spiritual heritage to share God's
Bliss—divine peace, love, and joy. In prayer we enter the
mood of divine joy by saturating our consciousness with
loving thoughts of God.

Have you ever wondered why Jesus specifically said, "Give
us this day our daily bread"? He was reminding us that each
day we need to come to God and open ourselves to God's
bread, or blessing. Daily we have to renew our relationship
with God. We have a daily commitment to commune
with God.

We can observe the same law of daily fulfillment on the
physical level. Our body can use only a certain quantity
of food each day. Even though our pantry contains an
abundance of food, we can use only enough for each
day's needs.

God's infinite abundance already exists in this cosmic pantry.
Nonetheless, it is a spiritual law and requirement to ask God
for daily sustenance; for only by asking do you set in motion
the law of abundance in your individual life. God's grace

can only manifest through you in response to your heartfelt receptivity. Furthermore, by daily approaching God in prayer and meditation, you maintain your spiritual relationship with God and grow in the life of grace.

Praying daily for God's sustenance also develops in us a deeper awareness of our dependence on God as the source of all good in life. It is important that we acknowledge God as the sole source of our daily needs. *I have put my trust in You, O all-loving Father, O all-loving Mother. You alone know what I need for my well-being, physically, mentally, materially, spiritually. Therefore, daily I appeal to You, my Life, my Strength, my All.*

Another beautiful truth is hidden in the asking for bread daily. As our awareness of God unfolds, our needs and desires change. Former personal demands are renounced and replaced by the need to respond more fully to God's purpose and plan to fulfill Itself through us. Today we may need the bread of peace, and tomorrow perhaps the bread of faith, or greater harmony and forgiveness. Thus it is evident that our daily needs for God's sustenance change day by day.

Now let us consider the meaning of bread itself. Jesus spoke repeatedly of this sacred bread. On one occasion he said, "I am that bread of life. Your fathers did eat manna in the wilderness, and are dead. This is the bread which cometh down from heaven, that a man may eat thereof, and not die. I am the living bread which came down from heaven: if any man eat of this bread, he shall live for ever." [13]

Jesus also said, "Verily, verily, I say unto you, Moses gave you not that bread from heaven; but my Father giveth you the true bread from heaven. For the bread of God is he which cometh down from heaven, and giveth life unto the world." [14]

These statements can also be understood in a purely mystical way—life itself is the bread. Life is bread. It is this mystical bread that Jesus spoke of when he said, "I am the bread of life." This "I" is not the personal "I," not Jesus the human being, but the I AM presence, which is the Christ, or the God-consciousness within him.

Think of it in this light. What really is bread for this body? What sustains the body? In yoga this sustenance is known as prana. Science terms it energy. Prana is the cosmic life force, the primeval, all-pervading energy. In religion it is sometimes called the life or the eternal existence of God. Prana is the sustaining power or bread of the body. Daily we need to be replenished with this prana, or living energy.

Whatever food is consumed is bread for the body, because its essence is prana, or cosmic life energy. It is not the form or the particular item of food that sustains you, but prana within it.

It is vitally important to offer grace, either vocally or silently, at mealtimes or at anytime food is taken. By offering grace, we acknowledge that God is the giver of the food as well as the essence of the food. Krishna says in the *Gita* that God, Brahman "is the offering, Brahman is the oblation...and one who performs the act of offering is also Brahman." [15]

By acknowledging that God is the source, the essence, and the bestower of all sustenance, we experience more fully God's presence and activity in us. When we offer grace with complete attention, we spiritualize or purify the food that is taken into the system by raising its vibration so that it has a beneficent effect on the whole person.

Let us suppose that we have taken care of all the physical needs of our body by giving it daily bread. What other needs remain? The needs of the mind; for the mind requires the bread of mental food.

What is this mental food or bread? Good thoughts. Godly thoughts are sustenance of the mind. Human or intellectual thoughts do not sustain the mind, for mind must have the living bread of God-thoughts.

Jesus recognized the spiritual importance of providing the mind with spiritual thoughts, when he said, "Blessed are they that do hunger and thirst after righteousness: for they shall be filled." [16] And when we are filled with right thoughts, or God-thoughts, we are indeed content and have mental peace.

Our heart also has a need for nourishment. And what is the

bread of the heart? We may have lots of wonderful ideas; we may be familiar with many philosophies; we may have memorized the Scriptures; we may be filled with marvelous information. But what good is all that knowledge of the mind if the heart is not nourished?

When we love everyone with our soul, we are feasting on the bread of the heart. All noble expressions of love sustain the heart, such as devotion, sympathy, patience, forgiveness, forbearance, and understanding. The heart of a human being must have the living bread of love in order to expand into the feeling of spiritual kinship with all life.

In addition to spiritual sustenance or love for the heart, we also need nourishment for our soul. Even though we may feel love for our fellow beings, we remain incomplete until our soul is filled with the unconditional love of God. The bread for our soul is God-consciousness, or the realization of divine Bliss. When we partake of that bread, we will share in the same spiritual attainment that was experienced by Krishna, Moses, Buddha, Christ, St. Francis, and Ramakrishna, as well as all illumined souls. Such is the blessedness and the transforming power of God's daily bread.

Forgive Us Our Debts as We Forgive Our Debtors

Meditation

The love for all beings leads us to the realization of oneness with all souls. Unless we first establish our hearts on that oneness, our human expressions of love will remain fragmented and disappointing.

We establish our consciousness on love through meditation. Spiritual life begins with meditation, because the regular practice of meditation lifts our minds and hearts, our whole consciousness, to God.

No one can live without God. Even if we claim, "Thank you, I am doing very well without God," we are deluding ourselves; for without God there is no life and no inner joy. God is life itself. None can live without the love of God, because God is the reality of love. We cannot live without ultimately turning our minds to God, because God is the Consciousness that sustains the mind. The way to turn our minds to God is through meditation.

Meditation is worship. Those who believe that religious worship simply means attending church have yet to realize the truth. True worship takes place in a temple not made with hands. The true devotee can worship God anywhere, since worship is personal communion with God, or subjective awareness of God revealing Itself to us. Only as we commune subjectively with God as the indwelling Presence are we worshiping God in spirit and in truth. Thus true worship is not dependent on being in a particular house of worship.

No one can know the truth for us. The messengers of truth remind us that each one must know the truth for himself or herself. Although the messengers have told us about the truth, their lives demonstrate that the truth can only transform us spiritually if we ourselves allow the truth to free us from ignorance, delusion, and self-limitation.

None of us is free until we attain spiritual freedom. Although human-created laws attempt to grant us freedom, these laws cannot assure freedom to anyone, because human-created laws are imperfect and changeable. Is it any wonder then that the Christ stressed the importance of attaining spiritual freedom through the transforming and liberating power of Truth? The ultimate freedom is our realization of spiritual perfection.

Worship is unfolding the divinity that is within us to its ultimate perfection. We do not *acquire* divinity or God-consciousness. There are no private or public correspondence courses that can guarantee us spiritual enlightenment and Self-liberation. Only a personal experience or direct knowledge of God can anoint us with the spirit of freedom.

We cannot approach God with any kind of bargaining consciousness. There is absolutely nothing of a material nature we can offer to God, for God doesn't need *things*. "Neither is [He] worshipped with men's hands, as though he needed any thing, seeing he giveth to all life, and breath, and all things...." [1]

If we hope to approach God, we must do so with love in our hearts. What we can offer to God is our love, which is always an acceptable gift unto God. The more we love God, the more God grants us the awareness of God's love for us.

What we need to unfold is the consciousness of our immortal nature. Do you realize that within you is the glorious Presence that is actually aching to be born, to manifest itself in your life? We suffer so long as we rebel against this spiritual birth. The Divine is always standing at the door of your heart, knocking again and again to be heard and to be allowed to enter. "Behold, I stand at the door, and knock: if any man hear my voice, and open the door, I will come in to him, and will sup with him, and he with me." [2]

There will always be an undercurrent of pain until we have come to God. If we take time to reflect, we will become aware that in the midst of all our objective pleasures and pursuits we are often restless and discontented. Yet we continue to believe that happiness will be ours if we have the fulfillment of our objective desires, such as a family, a fine home, financial security, membership in the "right" clubs and organizations—in short, "the good life." Thus human beings are perpetually preoccupied with worldly pursuits and possessions, forgetting that it is this continual busyness that prevents us from discovering our true Self, God within us.

Without God we will always feel this restlessness, and nothing of this world can assuage it. Even though we know the world cannot give us peace and contentment, we continue believing that it can. We continue to hope that someday, somehow, the world will fulfill our expectations. It never happens.

Our experiences in the world ultimately lead us to the discovery that our search must go back to the Source within us. God is the Source, which embodies within It all that we need for our life. This Source, the kingdom of God, is within you! Christ specifically said that this spiritual kingdom is *already* within us, not that it will be or may be. Hence, it is possible for us to discover it at any moment.

God's kingdom is *eternally* within us to provide for us, yet we still look for our provision to the kingdom of this world. When we put the world before God, we are living life backwards. We are seeking nourishment from the shell instead of looking for the food inside. Meditation teaches us how to get inside the shell, how to draw sustenance forth from within the Self, our creative consciousness.

In this world we will always have challenges and difficulties. Jesus told us that, "In the world ye shall have tribulation: but be of good cheer; I have overcome the world." [3] These tribulations have their value, and they work together for our good, if we understand their relationship to our total growth. If we look to the Self, God within, and pray for direction and strength, the Self will empower us to overcome all our difficulties and hardships. Even Jesus recognized our need to face these difficulties instead of trying to escape them: "I pray not that thou shouldest take them out of the world, but that thou shouldest keep them from the evil." [4]

All our challenges, difficulties, and obstacles are resources for the development of our spiritual integrity, moral fiber, and constructive physical action. We can use our obstacles constructively by constantly following God's guidance.

Suppose you have an apple with a small bad spot. Are you going to throw it away, thinking that the whole apple is rotten? Or will you look at the whole apple and cut out the infected part? Our life should be viewed as an integral whole, rather than as a series of fragmented episodes and experiences. For example, if we treat our mistakes as disasters rather than as means of growth, we become unduly distressed and negative. The moment we can relate every action to God, or the ultimate goal, we find ourselves inwardly strengthened and encouraged so that we can overcome the caviling tendency of the mind to dwell on past mistakes.

A mistake can be defined as a temporary misjudgment or false assessment of a situation. Spiritually, a mistake is an activity that does not express the highest level of discrimination. This morbid preoccupation with past mistakes imprisons people within their self-limitations and immobilizes their growth.

Meditation strengthens from within because it establishes our consciousness on the foundation of our existence—the reality of soul, on the attributes of soul that constitute the treasures of the kingdom of God within us. Let us put God first, and divine order will govern our life with its diverse activities. If we fail to establish our mind on God through effective prayer and meditation, we deprive ourselves of right understanding, enlightened perception, and unselfish conduct.

If we put God first in our life, our day will invariably begin with the thought of God and the remembrance of our inseparable oneness with God. Why should we doubt our real oneness with God, or be frightened of its possibility? If we are frightened or in doubt regarding our achieving God-consciousness, we are the victims of deeply engraved and false worldly beliefs and superstitions. Ignorance is at the root of our insistence on maintaining a distinction and sense of separation from God. Only the deluded human intellect claims that we are eternally separated from God. The enlightened Master urges us: "Be ye therefore perfect, even as your Father which is in heaven is perfect." [5] Surely the testimony of Jesus the Christ is to be trusted more than human interpretations of his teachings.

In meditation we are reminded to: "Be still, and know that I am God." [6] Have you reflected why it does not say, Be still, and know that *you* are God? If the Psalmist had written that, he would not have been expressing the highest truth. The I AM within you is God, not *you*—not the physical self, the mind, or the ego.

When we have learned to still all the thought-waves in the mind, we can go beyond the mind itself to discover the I AM presence, the real consciousness, or God-consciousness. The true I AM reveals itself only in the Silence. What is the Silence? The Silence is not the absence of noise, but the dynamic state of total Self-awareness. It is a state of calm, yet intense, inward alertness. It is infinite, not created; active, not passive; creative, not static. The Silence is Self-sufficient. It depends on nothing external to Itself. "Brahman is Silence," declares the *Chandogya Upanishad.*

When the I AM is realized in the Silence, there no longer is a *you*. The *you* of body-consciousness has disappeared. The *you* of sense-identification is dissolved. There is only the one I AM—the Soul, the Self, God the absolute One. God individualized within us is called the Soul, or Self. The same absolute God pervading the universe is the immanent Reality manifesting throughout creation. And the same God, beyond God's manifestation, beyond all forms and appearances, is God the Absolute.

When we know ourselves as the I AM, we are conscious of the presence of God as the only Reality. At all times the I AM is our true Guru, guide, and spiritual Master, and it shows us how to live each moment of our daily life. Let us remember that the I AM presence is the supreme Guru within every being.

The true mystic or yogi lives from within and always is conscious of the I AM, the divine presence, harmony, and oneness. Mystics do not concern themselves with psychic phenomena nor do they seek supernatural experiences. A true mystic feels the presence of God within oneself, and throughout the whole universe. By meditation the mystic transcends the senses, mind, intellect, and ego and merges with the transcendental Reality— Consciousness-Existence-Bliss Absolute.

Mystics may be found in any religion, although they are not confined by dogma. Whether they are called mystics or yogis makes no difference, for they have trod the same path, climbed the same mountain, and attained the same summit of Self-realization. Having realized God within

their inmost being, they have discovered the same God
to exist within all creation. Since every being possesses the
same potential spiritual awareness, everyone will ultimately
achieve the mystic union. Then why should we, who are
immortal children of Bliss, doubt our spiritual nature,
heritage, and destiny? As an ancient sage taught: "With
adoration and humility meditate upon Brahman, the source
and support of your mind and being. O ye embodiments
of divine perfection, ye sons of immortality, listen!" [7]

The Lord's Prayer is the prayer of a mystic. To understand
the meaning of this prayer, we have to enter into the spirit
of it; that is, we have to pray in the Spirit. Only by entering
into the consciousness of the Lord's Prayer with total love
and devotion are we transformed from within. Then it
will be possible for us to experience inwardly companionship
with the Master who shared this prayer with humanity.
By living the Lord's Prayer, we can attain the same state
of Christ-consciousness that Jesus realized and enter into
communion with all Masters who have manifested the
Christ-consciousness, or God-consciousness.

Let us remember that Jesus had to attain Christ-
consciousness for himself. At birth he was given the name
Jesus. It was only when he attained God-consciousness
that he became known as "the Christ," a term that is
derived from the ancient Greek word Christos, meaning
"the Anointed." The word Christ can be traced back
further to the Sanskrit Christna, or Krishna. Therefore

he should be referred to as Jesus the Christ, or Jesus of Christ-consciousness.

Buddha was not baptized Gautama Buddha. The prince Gautama became the Buddha, or the Enlightened One, when he attained God-consciousness, or Nirvana. Zoroaster was not baptized Zoroaster. He was given the name Spitama at birth and became Zoroaster when he attained the realization of God, or Ahura Mazda, the Supreme Light. Zoroaster was also known as Zarathustra, which means "he of the golden light, he of the supreme effulgence." One who has attained the supreme illumination of God becomes a Zarathustra, a Buddha, a Christ.

Forgive Us Our Debts as We Forgive Our Debtors

Did you ever wonder why Jesus, having attained Christ-consciousness, included himself when he prayed, Father, "forgive us?" Why did he need to ask for forgiveness? By including himself in his prayer for forgiveness, he reflects a measure of his true greatness—his humility and his oneness with humanity. A being of lesser spiritual stature might have stood off and prayed, "forgive them."

A tragic pattern of separating the spiritual from the worldly life has crept into religion. Why should there be any separation at all? Why shouldn't the expression and evidence of our spiritual life permeate every activity of our worldly life? When we spiritualize our thinking, we live in the consciousness that nothing is ever separate from God.

Some people who claim to be religious believe themselves to be more righteous and knowledgeable than others who attend their own church or belong to another faith and worship in an unfamiliar manner. Their false piety shows a lack of true charity and spiritual understanding toward others. Devastatingly blind to their own faults, they are nonetheless quick to see the faults of others and to judge them harshly. Those afflicted with the holier-than-thou consciousness are denied the grace of heaven.

Those who are unable to forgive others alienate themselves from their brother and sister beings. They commit the most heinous injury of all, for they impute to others the faults that they bear in their own impure minds.

To the pure, all things are pure. To the lover of God, all paths to God are good and true. To the unrighteous and impure mind, the paths that others follow are judged as unrighteous or inferior. Jesus set a supreme example. He never claimed to be holier than, or superior to, others, nor did he set himself apart from others, but he prayed, "forgive us."

What need did Jesus have to pray for forgiveness? The unconditional love of God flowed unceasingly through his being so that the spirit of self-sacrifice and self-surrender qualified him to serve humankind. He sought nothing for himself. He renounced personal family ties so that he could give himself totally to humanity and an extended spiritual family. When he prayed for forgiveness, he revealed his profound spiritual understanding and compassion for all erring humanity.

Jesus was not unlike his human brothers and sisters, for he, too, had weaknesses and knew the temptations of the flesh and the ego. How can anyone be tempted unless there is some weakness? We know that he had subjective struggles and moments of despair when he himself did not feel God's presence. Recall his anguished cry on the cross, "My God, my God, why hast thou forsaken me?" [8] before he regained the conscious awareness of God's loving nearness and protection.

His struggles endear him all the more to us and offer encouragement and strength because we see he was a man who conquered all self-limitations and weaknesses. The more we triumph over our own weaknesses, the less we are apt to condemn the weaknesses of others.

Jesus did not censure Mary of Magdala as did her accusers, for he loved her. Then why should we judge or condemn our human brothers and sisters? Let us examine our own actions and thoughts, and we shall find sufficient reason to suspend judgment and to purify our own hearts. Although Christ did not condemn Mary of Magdala, he did give her a commandment: "Go and sin no more." [9] If we insist on repeating our mistakes and indulging our weaknesses, we have only ourselves to blame for the consequences. Our sufferings result from the ignorance, negligence, and misuse of spiritual laws.

Jesus understood human nature. He was aware that we do not always find it in our hearts to forgive the errors of one another, even our own family and friends. So he taught us to turn to the all-loving Father, who is the ocean of forgiveness. He knew that the nature of God is to manifest itself as forgiveness in human life. When the Christ prayed, *Father, forgive us*, he revealed that he lived in unbroken communion with the Source, God the Father, God the Mother.

In his infinite compassion, Jesus also understood that often we cannot forgive ourselves for our own shortcomings and weaknesses. Selfish or thoughtless actions result in feelings of remorse and guilt, and we suffer. Even if we try to rationalize our own unrighteous actions by observing them in others, a part of us still feels guilty. No peace can come so long as there is any trace of negativity or judgment.

Negativity is an assault on our true nature—our spiritual Self. So long as we harbor negative feelings, we remain in conflict with the truth of our being, and we suffer. Through suffering, we are eventually impelled to reach out beyond our limited self to the spiritual consciousness that is free from all suffering.

Jesus evaluated all his experiences, both pleasurable and

painful, in the light of God. Therefore, he could pray, Father, forgive us, because he realized that God alone can truly forgive when we surrender to God. He recognized our capacity to receive God's forgiveness and that none can know peace without divine grace.

When we sincerely pray *Father, forgive us, Mother, forgive us*, our consciousness is lifted beyond self-limitation. Our consciousness becomes centered in God when we unite ourselves with God. Then we experience the response of unconditional love as evidence of total forgiveness.

The key to the practice of forgiveness is found in the word itself. "To forgive" means "to give for," that is, to replace a negative quality or condition by a positive or spiritual action. For example, for weakness, give strength. For harshness, give kind words. For impatience, give patience. For anger, give understanding. For hatred, give love.

Always remember to forgive yourself. If unrighteous thoughts appear, give your mind the nourishment of good thoughts. If negative emotions strike you, give yourself positive feelings of love and good will. Be gentle and patient with yourself. Give thankfulness for ingratitude because it is a privilege to give without any expectation to receive. Remember that an ungrateful heart is a curse unto itself. Be thankful for everything that you do have instead of dwelling on what you have not. As you reflect on your own blessings and rejoice in the blessings of others, you experience a greater awareness of God's grace in your daily life. That is living in the blessed consciousness of forgiveness.

The most sublime experience of forgiveness is this: that in place of the consciousness of conflict and unhappiness, God bestows on us the grace of love and harmony. When the consciousness of divine unity is attained, the flowering of joy and bliss follows spontaneously, and we are inevitably released from our self-limitations.

The all-loving God of forgiveness is found in the sanctuary of our innermost being. We need, therefore, to turn inward to the Source to gain the experience of forgiveness.

Why do we first have to forgive ourselves? So that we may experience true forgiveness. Only then can we reach out in forgiveness to our neighbors. This forgiveness is achieved through the practice of self-giving love, active devotional prayer, untying the knots of the heart, and by replacing our negative thought-waves with positive thought-waves. When the thought of our "enemy" wells up in the mind, let us immediately try to immerse ourselves in the positive qualities of that individual. No doubt this is a difficult exercise at first when we feel terribly wronged, but it is essential for the maturing process.

If you succeed in perceiving even one ennobling quality in the other, then it will open your vision to behold even more admirable characteristics than you thought yourself capable of recognizing. If you continue with this practice in forgiveness, it will awaken in you an actual feeling of good will toward the other and harmony within yourself. Never forget that whatever thought you broadcast to others comes back to you. Whatever unrighteous thought you harbor about your neighbor becomes an indictment against yourself and becomes the seed for personal suffering.

The whole secret of forgiving is really doing unto others what you would have them do unto you—and doing unto yourself what you would do unto others. You cannot practice the one without applying the other as well.

Jesus' whole concept of religion was predicated on the divinity of humankind. Had he believed that we are essentially finite or inherently sinful, do you think he could have given us the Lord's Prayer, which reveals our potential to become freed from "evil" or "sin?" Look at the lofty concept Christ had of humankind in recognizing that even the most self-degraded human being can find a way back to God, our all-loving Father, our Divine Mother. Surely he would not have prayed, "Father, forgive us," unless he believed in every human being's capacity to experience forgiveness. We are all worthy of the Divine's forgiveness, because we are God's children and God loves us.

Swami Premananda has defined true forgiveness, which unifies humankind, as "the awakening of divinity in another, by the manifestation of one's own."

Now let us consider what Jesus meant when he specifically prayed for forgiveness of our "debts." In our worldly transactions, debts refer to our financial obligations. Jesus, however, was speaking of our spiritual debts, that is, our spiritual obligations that have to be fulfilled. Spiritually, we are asking forgiveness for two kinds of debts: our debts to God and our debts to humankind.

Did you ever ask yourself, What debts do I have to God? Notice that Jesus did not say forgive us our debt, but our debts. How many debts do we have to God? Indeed, we are indebted to God for everything: this very earth with its light, its mountains and streams, its oceans with their abundance, the fields with their plenitude, the glories of scripture and science, music and medicine, art and literature, family and friends. We cannot give anything to another except what God makes available to us to share with others. It is our privilege to be a channel for the outpouring of God's blessings on humankind.

Our primary debt to God is the remembrance of God in all things. If we forget God, we also forget our personal relationship to God. Then we forfeit the opportunity to be channels of service and to fulfill God's divine purpose for us, namely, to share God's nature and blessings with each other. The allegory of Adam and Eve in Genesis preserves this lesson of our forgetfulness of God as the source, sustenance, and the only law of abundance and creativity throughout the universe.

When we fall in consciousness or fail to remember our spiritual identity with God, we reap pain and suffering, as well as all other human discords. Thus we incur the debt of correcting this forgetfulness by rising again to God-consciousness. Our human miseries are not the outcome of God's negligence, partiality, judgment, or punishment, but of our falling away in consciousness from our spiritual nature of absolute perfection.

O Lord, I have forgotten You. Help me remember my divine origin, that You are my creator, that You are the Father, the Mother, the Infinite, that in You I am alive and perfect. Let me never again forget You as the only creative power, presence, law, sustainer, and guide. Let me ever remember that You are all in all, and the fulfillment of all spiritual desires and visions.

Jesus praises the Father most gloriously by saying "our Father." He remembers his divine origin and includes us in this divine remembrance. Like Christ, we, too, are the holy children of the same God. As long as the children of God seek God, the Divine Parent-child relationship is sustained. God sends us out into the world, God's creation, projection, and expression, that through it we may remember God and our conscious oneness with God's grace. We have come to unfold our spiritual consciousness and to encourage and inspire other seekers to achieve the same realization. Through this constant identification with the Divine, we realize our oneness with God. All

relationships with God ultimately complete themselves
in this divine identity.

Let us remember that in whatever way we relate to God,
be it as a child to God the Father or Mother, or to Love,
Wisdom, or Life, they all culminate in the divine reunion
of Soul with the Absolute.

Another debt we owe to God is the remembrance of our
divine relationship with God, God's creation, and God's
created. Everything that we perceive in this realm is the
Divine made visible. *O God, forgive me for forgetting to
perceive Thee in all and to behold all in Thee. Help me remember
that this is Thy creation, and that it follows Thy law of spiritual
evolution. Let me always remember that, "Everything is the
manifestation of God, the divine Reality."* [10] One proof that
we have forgotten this divine relationship between God
and God's creation is evidenced in our exploitation of
nature, even as a proof of divine remembrance is that
we learn to love everyone as part of our Self and ultimately
as one with our expanded cosmic Self.

Another spiritual obligation to God is to remember
that God dwells within us. I have forgotten that God is
within me; therefore I seek for God in a limited way in the
physical world around me or in other relative planes of
existence. *Help me, O God, to remember that You are within
me as my own Soul. Guide me to remember that I am not the body
but the ever free Spirit, the ever pure, and ever perfect Soul.*

I have a debt to God because God has given my Soul the materials to create a body so that my Soul may be adorned with a physical garment. To express itself on the physical plane, Soul requires a spiritual sanctuary. Wist ye not that your body is the living temple of God? When we desecrate, defile, or misuse the body, then we have forgotten its divinity.

My mind also has a debt to God. One vital function of the mind is to remember that God is the source of its light of intelligence and all its noble and creative expressions. By offering all our thoughts to God, we repay our mental debt to God. Another very important function of the mind is to dwell on the spiritual qualities, the good, the true, and the beautiful. That is how our mind remembers God and thus goes back to God.

In discharging my debts to God, I have to remember, above all, that I am not the ego—the sense of a selfhood apart from God—but the Soul, ever identical with God. Only through self-delusion do we imagine that we exist and function independent of God. We forget God every time we cater to the ego, to sense-gratification, mental arrogance, emotional vanity, and psychological rationalization of selfish behavior. We have encouraged the expansion of the ego with all its self-indulgences, immature values, and prejudices, instead of nourishing our life with spiritual values and unselfish pursuits.

Help us, O God, to remember that we are not this finite, mortal, and imperfect self, or ego, but that we are the infinite, immortal, and perfect Self—omnipotent, omniscient, and omnipresent.

Our total debt to God is essentially the remembrance of God at all times and under all circumstances. We therefore need to manifest the divinity that is within us, by sharing our innate divine qualities with the whole universe. By attaining our conscious oneness with God, we fulfill our final debt to God.

Then what debts do we owe to our human brothers and sisters? How are we to take care of these debts?

Jesus the Christ showed us the way to absolve ourselves from our debts to others. Love your enemies. Bless them that curse you. Do good to them that hate you. Pray for them that despitefully use you and persecute you. [11]

We are to grow in love, we are to manifest goodness, we are to pray, and we are to bless everyone, especially our enemies.

How do we know that we have truly forgiven another who has injured us, physically, mentally, or emotionally? We know we are to love our enemy, but *how* to love our enemy? The scriptures of yoga and the teachings of the *rishis* provide very specific guidelines. We can only love our enemies when we recognize that there is only the one

Self, God, manifesting as each one of us. Therefore, our enemy is not really our enemy but our own self. In love there is the realization of oneness, and in this oneness, how can there be room for any thought of enmity?

There is a way to cleanse our mind and heart of all enmity toward another. Every time "the enemy" comes to mind, try to see God in him or her by contemplating that one's innate spiritual qualities until you actually feel forgiveness toward that one. This feeling of forgiveness will be an expression of the love of God in action.

Jesus perceived godliness in everyone, even in Judas who betrayed him, in Peter who denied him, and in Mary of Magdala who was confused and frightened. If someone betrays, denies, or condemns you, can you love him or her in spite of that unrighteous action? We are not asked to love unrighteousness but to love the innate divinity in humankind that transcends our actions. By identifying with the spiritual Self in others, we manifest more of our own spirituality. As a man thinketh in his heart, so is he.

The law of karma, cause and effect, operates impersonally in our experience. By condemning others, we condemn ourselves; we are, in fact, condemning God. Thus we create more karmic debts for ourselves. However, by blessing others, we free ourselves from our karmic debts and ascend in consciousness to that perfection of God, which is beyond karma.

Forgiveness requires patient and persistent practice, but it is the debt we owe to all beings. The acid proof that we have forgiven our enemy is that we no longer harbor any feeling of fear, hostility, or resentment toward that person whenever we think of that one. Such is the blessed power of practicing forgiveness.

Let Us Not Enter into Temptation/ Lead Us Not into Temptation

Meditation

Meditation is the foundation of yoga, therefore of our very life and well-being. Essentially, meditation is establishing our mind on God and keeping it centered in God, or the Infinite. Thus in meditation the possibilities of Self-discovery are inexhaustible.

Meditation is a specific practice with a specific ideal; although it is precise in application, it is infinite in expression. Meditation is the recognition that there is within me a Presence that is the ocean of beauty and harmony, of love, peace, and joy, of goodness, truth, and light, compassion and forgiveness—all that is beautiful and eternal.

The inner reality of meditation is perfectly expressed in the Old Testament: "Thou wilt keep him in perfect peace, whose mind is stayed on thee." [1] The phrase "stayed on thee," although archaic, emphasizes the ideal of meditation. When our mind is established, or stayed, on God, it means we abide in the meditative consciousness.

Whatever we meditate on continuously comes to pass in our experience. The fruits of meditation are inevitable. For example, if we keep the mind established on God, our godlike nature must unfold. The meditative mind reveals that we are created in the image of the eternal Reality, which is peace in its essence, joy in its fullness, love in its expression, and truth in its illumination. It is equally true that if we keep our mind stayed on the "world," then we will perpetuate worldly mindedness and self-limiting experiences.

In the life of a votary of truth, the spiritual takes precedence over the nonspiritual, because the spiritual is closer to the ultimate Reality, or the Source of our being. If we meditate on things that are of a secondary nature, then our life will be second rate; our experiences will be worldly, which means they will leave us incomplete, unfulfilled, and dissatisfied. But if we meditate on eternal values, then our experiences will be correspondingly meaningful, joyous, and expansive. Whatever we meditate on will externalize itself in our life in some way; such is the power of concentrated thought.

There is a story that illustrates the power of thought.
A young student could not concentrate on his lesson in
class. The teacher, who had been observing him for some
time, asked him, "Why aren't you paying attention?"
The young student, a simple farm boy, explained, "I have
a pet bull at home; while I am in school, he is all alone.
That makes me very sad. I miss him so much that I can't
think of anything else when I come to class."

The teacher was very understanding. Instead of sending
the pupil to the principal to be disciplined he said, "Why
don't you leave the class for a while? Go up the hill and just
meditate a little. Think about your reason for loving your
pet bull so much. Then come back to class."

The youngster spent seven days meditating on his pet bull.
When he returned to the school, he remained standing for
some time outside the classroom door. His teacher saw
him and requested him to come inside. The boy answered,
"I would like to come in, but I can't. My horns are too
long, and they won't fit through the doorway."

He had become so identified with the object of his affection
that he actually felt himself to be that object. In his mind
he took on the dimensions of the bull. Such is the power of
thought, that whenever we identify strongly with anything,
we absorb its characteristics.

Sometimes this principle of absorption can be observed in

the features of married couples. Instead of looking any longer like husband and wife (whatever that is supposed to mean), they look more like brother and sister, even in their gestures, mannerisms, and expressions.

Sometimes when we see a stranger walking down the street, we may get the definite impression that he is engaged in a particular occupation. Even without consciously trying to discover what he does, we receive a specific impression; because whatever he identifies with most in his daily life is vibrationally projected into the atmosphere, or environment.

If we understand this law of vibration, we can better appreciate the proverb, "Birds of a feather flock together." Therefore, we should associate with those of a similar constructive and harmonious orientation. There is real danger in associating with people of a gross and negative vibration, for we may very well be degraded by such contacts. If we choose spiritual companions, we will be spiritually benefited and uplifted in consciousness.

The enlightened ones, such as Krishna, Christ, Buddha, Shankar, and Chaitannya, all are in accord in teaching that devotees should keep company with the virtuous if they intend to make any progress on the spiritual path.

Unless one is firmly established on the spiritual path, contact with self-centered people may delude us into believing that their style of life is the right and natural way. Such false beliefs coarsen our feelings and thoughts. We delude ourselves if we believe that we are spiritually so advanced that we can freely mingle with the unrighteous without being contaminated by their actions. Only the Self-liberated have the spiritual strength and purity, not only to rise above all gross vibrations, but also to impart their spirituality to others.

Such is the power of thought that if we believe we are sinners, we will act "sinfully." However, if we believe that we are the holy children of God, then we will manifest godliness. The more we center our thoughts on God, the more we realize the nature of God.

If we believe we are separated from God, that we can never realize our oneness with God, that we are not good enough to know God, then we will *not* realize God. If we believe that we are not good enough to realize God, we will also believe that no one else is good enough to realize God. How true it is: "As [a man] thinketh in his heart, so is he." [2]

The most powerful degree of thought is meditation. Why? Because meditation reveals more and more of our eternal spiritual nature, our divine immortal attributes of Soul. As we think on these attributes, we unfold them. We cannot help but manifest our godly qualities, because Soul yearns to express and share its divinity.

We do not *become* spiritual or godly, we do not become one with God; but we realize that which already *is*: the Self that is beyond the veils of self-limitation and mental darkness. This ignorance of mind disappears when we perceive the light of Soul, the light of Truth.

Meditation unifies our mind with Soul, the inner Reality. Meditation makes us receptive to the Truth, which dispels the consciousness of self-limitation, mental darkness, and separation from God. We do not remove darkness by fighting or resisting it, but by manifesting the light that is within us. In the light there is no darkness. One who fears darkness walks in darkness. One who concentrates on the light lives in the light.

The philosophy of yoga is to seek the light of Truth. Yoga is positive, constructive, and creative in its philosophy and expression. More than ever, our world is in need of spiritual idealism, constructive thinking, and the unfoldment of our innate divinity. Meditation, an integral aspect of yoga, should be the very core of one's daily life. A day without meditation is like a day without light, without joy, without peace. Each day that passes without meditation exposes us to the phobias, fears, and delusions of the world. If we are not spiritually conscientious, we will be overwhelmed by the negative and destructive thinking of the worldly minded.

These negative conditions cannot touch you if you

contemplate the presence of God, which is your own true Self. The body goes, but the I AM abides. Outer conditions change, but consciousness remains. The forms of life pass away, they have their birth and death, pleasure and pain; but life itself flows on, for it is eternal. The objects of our love change as we grow and unfold, but love itself is eternal. Our true nature is eternality. All else belongs to the mutable, non-Self; it is in the domain of maya. Contemplate your true nature, for that alone is worthy of your thought and love. This is the ideal of meditation in yoga, the realization that "I am God, naught else but God." [3]

The Lord's Prayer is the sublime expression of our true nature. One who knows how to pray the Lord's Prayer realizes God. Even the twelve disciples, who were constantly with Jesus, had to learn how to pray it. Why didn't they know how to pray? Perhaps some of the disciples were still attached to the outer observances of religion and ritualistic prayers. Therefore they, like so many others, had not explored the nature and way of interior prayer. But those disciples who had become spiritually awakened felt an inner need to deepen their knowledge of God and to discover their personal relationship with God.

Having observed their master's profound spiritual communion with the Father, they, too, wanted to know God as he knew God within himself. Knowing their preparedness to receive the Word, their master then instructed them in the Lord's Prayer.

Let Us Not Enter into Temptation

Does God *lead* us into temptation? If we truly understand the *nature* of God to be all-loving, all-forgiving, all-pervading, can we then any longer believe or claim that God leads anyone into temptation?

A very precise verse in the Epistle of James says: "Let no man say when he is tempted, I am tempted of God: for God cannot be tempted with evil, neither tempteth he any man." [4] If James and the other disciples understood that truth, then surely their master bore witness to it in all its fullness. Knowing that God tempts no one, how do we account for the expression, "Lead us not into temptation"? Due to inaccurate translation of the original text, religion has perpetuated the false concept that God leads humans into temptation. In the original Aramaic, the meaning is quite different and correctly translates as, "Let us not enter into temptation," or, "Leave us not in temptation."

The real thought is, *O God, our Father, our Mother, Thou creative Spirit, Thou all-loving Spirit, do not allow me to fall into temptation. And if I have fallen into temptation, O Thou all-loving Grace, do not leave me in this state of temptation, but reveal unto me the way to free myself from all temptations.*

God does not lead anyone into temptation. It is we who are enticed by our own false desires and worldly mindedness and led astray by our own weaknesses. It is we, and we alone, that tempt ourselves, and not God. Yet for thousands of years human beings have prayed as though God leads us into temptation. What kind of God would lead anyone into temptation? There is no such God and never has been, for God is pure, unconditional Love.

When you offer this prayer, never again allow yourself to pray to God, "Lead us not into temptation." Be subjectively aware that the true meaning of this expression is, "*Leave* us not in temptation." Though in public worship we may use the phrase "Lead us not into temptation," yet mentally and silently we pray, "Leave us not in temptation," or, "Let us not enter into temptation."

What exactly is temptation? Scripture records that Jesus was tempted like unto all human beings. He was tempted! Religion emphasizes that temptation means, "to be tried, to be tested." Who tests us, God? Never. The devil? Only if we believe in the devil.

Yoga is wonderful because it reveals to us the inner meaning of scripture in terms of our own inner illumination. The yogi recognizes all temptation to mean delusion. In the Lord's Prayer, temptation means delusion. Therefore the yogi prays, *O God, do not allow us to remain in the state of self-delusion. Do not let us live in ignorance. Do not let us remain in the consciousness of separation from Thee. Do not allow us to fall into still greater self-deception.*

Who of us can say that we are not tempted in life? Everyone encounters temptations and has to resolve them. Jesus recognized this truth himself; after all, he did pray, "Leave us not in temptation." He identified himself as part of every one of us. To each of us he was saying, "I, too, have known delusion and suffering. I, too, have known temptation in life. I am one of you."

At least four truths are revealed in that passage, "Leave us not in temptation." The first truth is that everyone who lives in this world suffers from self-delusion. It cannot be otherwise, because the nature of the world itself is delusion, or maya.

The next truth is that we can overcome our self-delusions, our false knowledge, our ignorance.

The third truth is that there is a way out of our delusion.

And the final truth is that the grace of God is the way. God's grace, love, and blessing are always available to us because the Infinite is all-pervading and the underlying principle of action throughout creation. God is not "out there," and we "over here." God is in the midst of us, God is within us; therefore God is ever with us. God is the activity of infinite love, life, and wisdom. In yoga this truth is called Sat-Chit-Ananda, or Consciousness-Existence-Bliss Absolute.

If the grace of God were not always available to us, we could not experience the truth of the Lord's Prayer. We could not be freed from self-delusion without the grace of God.

We speak of having many temptations, when in truth, there is only one basic temptation: the temptation to believe that there is a selfhood apart from God. Nevertheless, for purposes of discussion, temptation can be categorized into three aspects: temptation of the body, temptation of the mind, and temptation of the ego.

The life of Jesus offers a poignant illustration of the three temptations he had to transcend in order to attain Self-illumination and divine love; for only then could he be a guiding light unto the world. In St. Matthew 4:2-11 we read:

> And when he had fasted forty days and forty nights, he was afterward an hungered. And when the tempter came to him, he said, If thou be the Son of God, command that these stones be made bread. But he answered and said, It is written, Man shall not live by bread alone, but by every word that proceedeth out of the mouth of God.

> Then the devil taketh him up into the holy city, and setteth him on a pinnacle of the temple, And saith unto him, If thou be the Son of God, cast thyself down: for it is written, He shall give his angels charge concerning thee: and in their hands they shall bear thee up, lest at any time thou dash thy foot against a stone. Jesus said unto him, It is written again, Thou shalt not tempt the Lord thy God.

Again, the devil taketh him up into an exceeding high mountain, and sheweth him all the kingdoms of the world, and the glory of them; And saith unto him, All these things will I give thee, if thou wilt fall down and worship me.

Then saith Jesus unto him, Get thee hence, Satan: for it is written, Thou shalt worship the Lord thy God, and him only shalt thou serve.

Then the devil leaveth him, and, behold, angels came and ministered unto him.

The first temptation to turn stones into bread represents the temptation of the body, of the senses. Remember that this temptation came after forty days of fasting. We know that when we miss even one meal we are physically hungry. Can we then possibly imagine how intense must have been the hunger of Jesus after fasting forty days?

At this point of extreme hunger, the tempter appears. This tempter is also referred to as Satan, or the devil. What does the tempter symbolize? Satan, the tempter, is the personification of the ego-sense. The ego is our sense-identified self-consciousness, the unreal or noneternal self. It is this "I" consciousness that is solely occupied with its personal demands, needs, and desires. This finite "I" consciousness creates all self-delusions, temptations, and fears. Thus the tempter is never really an entity or a person but the personification of human beings' collective, finite, and negative impressions.

The ego appears in whatever guise appeals to our lower instincts or selfish desires. The ego seeks to create doubt in our mind and taunts us by saying, "*If* thou be the Son of God"—and this challenge is thrust upon every one of us. We *are* all Children of God! Even so, the tempter mocks us and encourages us to doubt our spiritual identity: "So you think you're the Son of God, the Daughter of God. Ha! Well, if you are, let's see what you can do with these stones. Can you change them into bread?"

Though Jesus, like other masters of yoga, possessed the psychic power to transmute one substance into another, he chose not to exercise this power rather than misuse it for self-glorification. He affirmed and acknowledged the power of God as the only real power and substance of life when he said, "Man shall not live by bread alone, but by every word that proceedeth out of the mouth of God." [5] In other words, we are not to live only by the effects, or phenomena of the world. They alone are not enough.

Let us carefully observe that Jesus did not reject or deny the need for the goods of this world. Rather, he acknowledged that these in themselves are not sufficient for our well-being. Our physical needs, represented by bread, must be supplemented by spiritual sustenance, which is expressed by "every word that proceedeth out of the mouth of God." Our real sustenance is spiritual, and it externalizes itself as that which is needed for our harmonious growth and Self-expression in this world.

The delusion of the physical body is the temptation to think that the body is the only reality, or that the objects or pleasures of the senses are the source of happiness. Is not this delusion itself the cause of human misery?

O God, do not let me remain in the delusion that anything of the phenomenal world can bestow contentment or bring fulfillment. Don't allow me to forget that Thou, the divine Reality, art the only source of peace and happiness.

Not only are we tempted to think we are physical beings; but also even more subtle is our temptation to regard our mind as the supreme power and reality in our lives. The arrogance of the intellect is symbolized in the temptation that comes to Jesus when he is set on the pinnacle of the temple and tempted to misuse the mental and psychic faculties for self-glorification. Jesus at once rejects this subtle temptation of the intellect to glorify itself. Those who succumb to this temptation are indeed self-deluded; yet they believe that their intellect is far superior to anyone else's and consequently they should be entrusted with the authority to dictate how others should live and behave.

The unenlightened mind suffers from the destructive delusion that the mind itself is the supreme power. However, to the awakened or the enlightened, the mind is recognized as being only an instrument for the expression of authentic power—the power of God, the only real power.

The mind would have us believe in two powers, which are in eternal conflict with each other. The human mind believes in having to overcome a power called "the world," or "matter," as in the expression "mind over matter," or as in good over evil. There is no mind over matter, or good over evil, except as creations or concepts of the mind itself. The finite mind fabricates the delusion that mind and matter, good and evil, are distinct realities. What is matter, but an externalization of Consciousness, even as the body is the physical manifestation of the Divine Mind, and human-made objects are the creation of human thoughts and imagination. Only in the state of self-delusion do we believe in a separation between Reality and Its manifestations.

Let us remember that mind as much as "matter" is still within a state of self-limitation, or duality. While in the state of duality the mind can only perceive good and evil, which are its own creations. Having projected these, we then believe that they are powers, and according to our belief, they *act* as powers.

In its ignorance and arrogance, the self-deluded mind is convinced that objective knowledge or book learning is the ultimate goal and achievement in life. Though book knowledge is important and invaluable to our intellectual development, it cannot confer enlightenment. Books can give information and inspiration; but no book has the power to bestow Self-realization.

One may have a great command of arts or sciences and be classified as a great intellect or scholar, without necessarily having any real understanding or warmth of heart for others. In such instances book learning, instead of expanding the mind, has enslaved it. *O Lord, don't let me fall prey to the temptation of believing that objective knowledge is the supreme power and goal of life. May I always remember that Thou art the author of the book of life itself, and therefore I must come to Thee for enlightenment and guidance.*

In the third temptation—the temptation of the ego— Jesus is taken to the top of an exceedingly high mountain. He is offered dominion over the world—that is, over all he perceives—if only he will acknowledge the ego as the supreme self.

Ego is concerned only with self-aggrandizement and the quest for personal power, without regard for the welfare of others. Ego is busily building walls of selfishness all around itself, and then it becomes trapped within its own boundaries of self-centeredness. The light cannot penetrate these walls of egotism.

Ego says to us all, "If you will fall down and worship me, if you will recognize only me—that is, if you will recognize only me, my demands, my wishes—then whatever you want will be yours." When we remember that whatever is gained selfishly by the activity of ego leads to the fear of loss and to personal misery, then we will not be deluded by the false promises of the ego. "For what shall it profit a man, if he shall gain the whole world, and lose his own soul?" [6] Of course, it is not that we can lose our soul, but we can lose the consciousness of being the soul. We can lose sight of the light, love, and wisdom of our soul when we put the ego and its demands first in our life. When we realize that, we can find inspiration in the revelation, "Thou shalt have no other gods before me." [7] Yet how often have human beings sold their soul for a little sensory gratification or lust for power, such as we find illustrated by Faust, who sells his soul to the devil in the old legend.

When tempted by the ego, the Master within us immediately responds with the thought expressed by Christ, "Thou shalt worship the Lord thy God, and him only shalt thou serve." [8] Then the ego, Satan, is forced to disappear, for in the presence of God-consciousness and God-power, the ego sense cannot function. Thus is dispelled the last temptation in a human being, the ultimate self-delusion that the ego is the source, sustenance, and fulfillment of life.

Then the angels came and ministered unto Christ. The angels personify our spiritual qualities. In Sanskrit the word corresponding to angel is *deva*, which means light, that is, spiritual light. Our God-given qualities are our

angels, which are always ready to minister unto us when
we acknowledge their presence. Ego, or the tempter,
strives to ensnare us in the delusion that it is the source of
power, peace, and success. Ego tempts us to imagine that it
is the light. If we see through the deceptions of the ego,
we can expose it and command it in these words: "Get thee
hence! I will not have any part of thee. None but God
will I love, serve, and acknowledge as the supreme power."
In this recognition, our inner spiritual treasures reveal
themselves to us.

The following story illustrates the power of truth over
the temptations of the ego, which here is referred to as the
devil. There was once a man whose practices aroused in
his mind the appearance of the devil. The man was delighted
to see the devil and exclaimed, "Oh, I have been trying so
hard to contact you. And now that you are here I have a
request. If you will fulfill my desires, I'll do anything
you want."

The devil said, "Yes, I can fulfill your desires, but there
is one condition. You must keep me busy all twenty-four
hours of the day. If you do not keep me constantly occupied,
I will devour you. I will take your life."

This greedy man did not regard the devil's demand as an
unreasonable condition to fulfill, so he agreed. Then the
devil said, "Now that we have made our contract, what do
you want?"

"Build me a palace," demanded the man. Immediately the palace materialized before him.

The devil asked, "What next?"

"Build me a road leading to the palace."
That, too, was done instantly; and again the devil urged the man to make his next request. The man thought, "My goodness, how is he getting this done so quickly? This devil is incredible. What can I require of him that will be more difficult and take longer?" After pondering for a moment, he demanded, "Build me a town." Although this task took a little more time, there was still the whole rest of the day ahead of him. The foolish man was becoming frantic and frightened, because he saw now that it would be difficult to keep the devil busy for the rest of time.

What to do to keep the devil occupied? The foolish one decided to seek out a holy man, and explained his dilemma. "What am I to do about this devil?" he pleaded. "He will kill me unless I keep him occupied all the time."

The holy man said, "There is a solution. This is what you must do. Take a bamboo cane, plant it in the ground, and order the devil to run up and down the bamboo cane until you have decided on his next task."

The devil had to do as he was commanded. He started going up and down this bamboo pole, and soon he became so bored and exhausted that he wanted to get as far away as possible. So he disappeared, never to return again.

If we envision the bamboo as the pole of meditation, and if we make our mantram run up and down our pole of meditation, our mind will be centered on God. Then the ego will not be free to dominate our life, but will be forced to leave. It cannot function in the consciousness that is established on God. The power of meditation dislodges the hold of the ego.

There are many mantrams, such as the Lord's Prayer and the ancient Vedic Prayer known as the Gayatri, as well as Hong Swa and Aum, meditations mentioned in the Upanishads. By profound subjective meditation on any one of these mantrams under qualified guidance, we can dispel the ego-consciousness because it cannot function in the light of Truth, in the presence of divine Love.

Deliver Us from Evil

Meditation

The love for all beings leads us to the realization of the Self, yet the mechanics of living keep us so busy that we tend to forget this most important purpose for living. We put our objective duties and pleasures first, and in our frenzy to carry out all the activities we plan for ourselves, we dissipate most of our energy during the day. We squander both mental and physical energy without any sense of direction.

We live in a frenzy because we have not learned how to direct our mind to do things in a natural yet orderly way, without tension, without loss of time, without dissipation of energy. Yoga is so vitally important to modern living because it shows us how to utilize every precious moment of our lives—and every moment is indeed most sacred. Yoga teaches us to live each moment creatively and calmly.

At the heart of the practice of yoga is the principle of being calmly active and actively calm under all circumstances. Once we begin to experience inner calm, we realize that we cannot live without yoga. By the practice of yoga our life becomes more meaningful and joyous—spontaneously joyous, subjectively joyous, permanently filled with a sense of peace, purpose, and well-being. Meditation is the fundamental means of achieving the inner state of peace that all human beings basically seek. In fact, meditation is the foundation of yoga, because it begins with the thought of God.

Every scripture of the world begins with the thought of God: "In the beginning, God...." The central theme in scripture is God—the nature of God—and the ways to realize God. Unfortunately, precept and practice do not always go hand in hand. We may read a few verses or a chapter from scripture each day; but as soon as our daily activities begin, we seem to forget the spiritual instruction of scripture. Actually, we have not forgotten the instruction; we have only failed to give proper reflection to it, and thus these truths are not absorbed into our consciousness.

Meditation reveals to us the inner meaning and personal application of scripture. If you read scripture as part of your daily devotions and then meditate on its meaning, you will discover its true subjective significance, either while meditating or later during your daily activities. If you faithfully and patiently continue your daily devotions and meditations, they will eventually bear much spiritual fruitage.

If we begin all our activities with the thought of God, our life will be transformed from self-centeredness to God-centeredness. The self-centered person is constantly occupied with the desire for self-gratification, with getting, possessing, and dominating; whereas the God-centered being is inwardly content and thinks of sharing and serving.

God-orientation is based on these thoughts: How can I more fully manifest the divinity within me? How can I be of greater service to my fellow beings? How can I help my family members spiritually, by helping them to unfold their innate divinity?

We help others spiritually by first manifesting our own innate divinity or spiritual perfection and then manifesting the light, love, and harmony that is innate and part of our spiritual heritage. We do not acquire spirituality, we simply uncover the spiritual perfection that is within us.

When Jesus gave us the commandment, "Be ye therefore perfect, even as your Father which is in heaven is perfect," [1] he meant exactly what he said. When we do not understand scripture, we behave like the preacher in the story who read aloud from the scripture during the sermon and said, "This verse doth not really mean what it saith."

Do not let us dismiss a verse as untrue because we do not understand it or because it does not agree with our understanding. Jesus did not say that you *may* be as perfect as your Father, or that you *might* become perfect; he reminds us to be as perfect as God is perfect. Human beings do not need to strive for perfection; we only need to manifest our innate perfection. Jesus sought to lift us to the truth of our spiritual perfection.

Jesus, who followed the guidance of God within himself, realized the highest truth equally inherent in all humankind. He never claimed that only one, or a few, could realize spiritual perfection, but encouraged all to regain the realization of their inherent perfection: "Be ye perfect."

There is a vast difference between *being* perfect and *becoming* perfect. To *become* means that we want to be something other than what we are; and it is philosophically impossible to turn into something we are not. To become also implies a sense of lack. To be perfect means we already are perfection, but we have yet to realize our perfection. We need to come into a personal awareness that we are the perfect Self, spoken of as God—beyond change, beyond becoming, beyond limitation.

To use an illustration: No matter how dusty and dirty a diamond may appear to be, when the grime is wiped away, the diamond reveals its pristine purity. It has not changed in any way, nor has it become pure. It has not acquired brilliance or beauty, for these qualities are inherent to its nature. They are simply uncovered by removing the dirt that has concealed its inherent perfection, its brilliance, its beauty. In the same way, we uncover the perfection or divinity already within us.

This is *being* perfect. Not only Jesus, but also other yogis and mystics have realized perfection and taught us to be perfect. Above all, God has inspired humankind to be perfect. God commanded Abraham, who represents every human being, to be perfect. Yoga itself means the realization of spiritual perfection, the realization of Soul's oneness with God.

This mystic union is beyond speech, beyond mind, beyond intellect, beyond duality. Therefore, we must transcend the consciousness and concepts of duality in order to enter into spiritual perfection. Although the highest truths cannot be expressed, we feel the need to use illustrations in an attempt to reveal the inexpressible.

For example, when Jesus sought to explain the kingdom of heaven he had to use similes, knowing that there were no words that would directly convey the truth. No wonder he said, "The kingdom of heaven is *like....*" and, "With what comparison shall we compare it?"

Thus Christ taught, "The kingdom of heaven is like to a grain of mustard seed, which a man took, and sowed in his field: Which indeed is the least of all seeds: but when it is grown, it is the greatest among herbs, and becometh a tree, so that the birds of the air come and lodge in the branches thereof." [2]

"Again, the kingdom of heaven is like unto a merchant man, seeking goodly pearls: Who, when he had found one pearl of great price, went and sold all that he had, and bought it." [3]

"Again, the kingdom of heaven is like unto a net, that was cast into the sea, and gathered of every kind: Which, when it was full, they drew to shore, and sat down, and gathered the good into vessels, but cast the bad away." [4]

A spiritual truth is like love, which can never be fully described although we seek to express it through our senses, mind, and heart. The essence of love transcends human expression and is realized in the Soul. If asked to describe the reality of love, we resort to comparisons or similes, such as, "It is like this, or it is like that," without ever succeeding in really expressing it. Why can love not be fully expressed? Because love is the realization of oneness, and whatever is expressed can only be a manifestation of that oneness.

That oneness is beyond the feeling of separation, division, or multiplicity. Beyond diversity is oneness, or perfection, which is infinite and formless. When Jesus pointed us to spiritual perfection, he sought to lift our vision beyond name and form, beyond duality, beyond separateness. In other words, spiritual perfection is realized within one's own consciousness, and it is this truth Jesus spoke of when he said, "The kingdom of heaven is like...."

When the contemporaries of Jesus heard him speak of the kingdom of heaven and the spiritual perfection of humankind, they accused him of blasphemy, for in their ignorance they were convinced that human beings and God could never be one and identical, let alone that we could be as perfect as God. When we live in the darkness of ignorance, in bondage to sectarian or dogmatic beliefs, we are incapable of considering humankind as being other than imperfect. Christ, like the illumined yogis of all times, realized our innate spiritual perfection and therefore encouraged us to become consciously aware of our spiritual nature and our oneness with God. Of course, we cannot comprehend the ideal of spiritual perfection so long as we are identified with our body or with the world. The human self perceives only constant change and therefore cannot cognize the changeless Reality, which alone can reveal spiritual perfection.

When Jesus urged us to "Be perfect," he referred to a state of being and consciousness that is eternal, changeless, and transcendental. This pure state of being is voiced as I AM.

Through meditation Jesus realized that we also can rise above all self-limitations, all physical consciousness, all sense identification, and all finite impressions stored in the subconscious, to discover that luminous Reality, which is each Soul in its infinite perfection.

Meditation makes the mind soar beyond the gravity of self-limitation and imperfection. To become firmly established in such meditation, we should set aside at least two periods a day, preferably upon arising in the morning before the mind is ensnared in daily activity, and before retiring at night to direct the subconscious mind to God during sleep. It is also of inestimable benefit to set aside a few minutes throughout the day for meditative recollection and contemplation. This practice will expand our awareness of the presence of God and will keep our mind full of calmness and peace.

Meditative persons are so attuned to the indwelling Reality that they constantly draw inspiration and guidance unto themselves for daily living. Uncover that ocean of perfection within you. Have recourse to it at all times. It will never fail you in its love, wisdom, and guidance. We are not meant to live in this world in the consciousness of imperfection, but to manifest and unfold the beauty, love, and perfection of God.

Deliver Us From Evil

As we ponder the Lord's Prayer, we become conscious of the spirit of profound humility from which it issues. Humility is a quality of soul. Humility is rooted in the spiritual perception of our essential identity and complete dependence on the all-loving Father-Mother God. Only the self-deluded intellect presumes to be self-sufficient and capable of being a law unto itself, whereas the pure of heart realize our spiritual kinship with all life and our true identity in God. This spiritual identity cannot be grasped by the senses; it is revealed through prayer and meditation. It alone deserves our total dedication and worship. The humble perceive unity in diversity and depend unfailingly on the ultimate Reality for wisdom, guidance, and Self-expression.

Humble persons never think only of themselves, but include all when praying to be freed from delusion or to be blessed by God. *O Father, O Blessed Mother, do not allow us to enter into the state of temptation, do not allow us to stay in the thought of limitation and separation. Do not allow us to live selfishly and fearfully, but "deliver us from evil"; for Thou alone art our Savior, our refuge, our source.*

What is the evil from which we pray to be delivered? Let us remember that Jesus included himself in this prayer, deliver *us*. He realized that no human being, regardless of spiritual stature, is completely free from the thought of evil, or negativity. Jesus acknowledged this powerful influence of negative thinking on the life of humankind. No wonder Jesus prayed for God to deliver humankind from its domination.

Let us consider the concept of evil, since there are many interpretations that we uphold in various societies. What is regarded as evil in one society may be acceptable as just and righteous in another. For example, adultery is considered an evil in some societies, but not in all. Killing is taught to be an evil, yet some societies accept it as justified. Since the concepts of evil vary with time, place, culture, and convenience, we have to delve deeper to understand the meaning of evil.

It becomes obvious that evil is, above all, a relative concept created by the human mind. Whatever the mind creates can only be finite and relative; it can never exist as an absolute. Once these concepts are created by the mind, we become the slave of our concepts. Therefore, we can be enslaved by our belief in evil, and we can be equally influenced by our belief in good. This recognition brings us to the understanding that both good and evil are relative concepts, and one does not exist or operate independent of the other.

Let us look at the word "evil" itself. What happens when you spell the word evil backward? "LIVE." Thus evil is the process of living life backward, that is, acknowledging any concept or form to exist apart from, or independent of, God, the absolute Perfection. Evil is believing that there is any power other than, or equal to, God. How could this be? Since God is omnipotence, can there be any other power?

The appearance of a power called evil existing apart from God is caused by self-delusion, ignorance, and false identification, which then manifest as our false beliefs. It is the false belief in anything existing apart from God that invests various forms with fear. That which brings fear or pain we call evil; that which causes pleasure and reduces pain we call good.

We see then that evil, as a *concept* enlivened by our belief that it has power, contains no truth, reality, or substance to support it. Evil cannot be an absolute, for God already is the Absolute. It is illogical and unphilosophical to postulate two absolutes, because they would cancel each other out. Likewise, two infinities cannot be possible, since one would be limited by the other. Furthermore, if evil were innately infinite and absolute, we could never be delivered from it, and Jesus' prayer would have been irrational and in vain.

How then are we to be delivered from evil? First we must understand that evil is a concept that is impermanent; it ceases to function when we realize that it is powerless in the presence of God. We need to be delivered from the evil that parades as ego-consciousness. It has been personified in the scriptures of mankind as Satan, devil, tempter, Mara, and Ahriman.

Christ himself had to dispel evil from within his consciousness. His struggle took him into the wilderness, a very appropriate symbol for the unenlightened mind. Only when Jesus realized the truth about evil, or Satan, was he able to free himself from its tantalizing appearance and alluring promises. Like Christ, every human being has to overcome the delusions of the body, mind, and ego, before it is possible to emerge as an illumined Child of God and minister unto our sisters and brothers.

So long as we think of evil as power, we will be locked in violent combat with it. However, when we learn not to resist evil but to overcome it by knowing the truth about it—namely, that it is *non*power, since God is the only power—then we are delivered from the consciousness, or concept, of evil.

When we look at the whole passage, "Let us not enter into temptation, but deliver us from evil," we are filled with renewed hope, assurance, and optimism that the power, love, and grace of God are always available to us if we open our consciousness to them and devote ourselves wholeheartedly to their manifestation.

Jesus has revealed to us the truth that the root of temptation is ego-consciousness, or our sense of a selfhood apart from God. Every spiritual master or enlightened yogi has taught the world this truth: It is the ego, born of ignorance, that is our real enemy and the progenitor of all unrighteousness and misery.

O Father, O Blessed Mother, let us not remain in this self-enslaving delusion that we are ever apart from You, or that there is anything outside of You that can have power over us; but free us from all spiritual ignorance, mental delusions, and self-deceptions. Deliver us by bringing to our conscious awareness the remembrance that You are ever with us because You are within us as the one and only unchanging, all-wise, all-loving presence of unconditional power and perfection. Amen.

When we realize that the ego is at the root of our personal attachments, delusions, and fears, we will never again allow ourselves to be dominated by the concepts of duality, the sense of separateness from God, or the belief in any person, place, or condition having power over us other than God. Nothing whatsoever, per se, can be evil, for everything in creation is the manifestation of the divine Reality. God alone is real. "The unreal hath no existence. The real can never cease to be. The seers of truth have realized the ultimate nature of both." [5] Because Jesus had realized this truth, he attained Christhood, nirvana, or samadhi—all names for the realization of spiritual perfection.

There is a little story of a minister that illustrates that the ego is humankind's greatest problem. A minister, well advanced in years and about to retire from the ministry, was asked, "What has been the greatest problem in your ministerial life?"

The minister instantly answered, "Myself."

The minister's observation is equally true for all of us. Our problem is not really anyone "out there," but "in here," existing as our sensory, or egotistic, self. Once we get beyond the consciousness that we are the finite self, we then free ourselves from the temptations of life, which only exist so long as there is ego-consciousness.

It is vitally important, therefore, to associate with those who are motivated by the desire to realize spiritual perfection. Narada, the ancient exponent of Bhakti yoga in India, taught us to shun all "evil" company by associating with the saints and other devotees of God. Buddha also taught that if a person could not find spiritual companionship, it would be better to walk alone on the path than to keep company with the unrighteous.

Let us remember that the ego sense exists not only within ourselves, but also in everyone else as well. It is difficult enough to cope with one's own ego manifestations. Then why subject ourselves to others who are engrossed in their egotism? Until we realize spiritual perfection, we remain under the influence of temptation, even as by wading in muddy water the body becomes covered by mud. However, if we step into clean water, the body will remain clean.

Of course, we acknowledge the truth that God dwells within all beings as the pure Self and that God is the all-pervading Reality. But as Ramakrishna wryly observed, although God dwells within all creatures, we should not try to hug the tiger, which does not have the realization that God dwells in it, or that it is a manifestation of God. Once we have become free from the entrenched belief of separateness from God, we can transcend the negativity of others and impart the power of spiritual purity to them.

In addition to keeping company with the virtuous as a means of freeing ourselves from negative influences, we must liberate our mind from its deeply embedded negative impressions. We must observe carefully what thoughts we entertain, what thoughts companion us throughout the day. Should impure thoughts dominate our mind, we are responsible for releasing them. But how?

Whenever any negative impression intrudes into our thinking, instead of resisting it, reacting to it, or fearing the impression, we should immediately remind ourselves that these impressions can no longer exercise any power over us because they have no spiritual law to support them. Self-deliverance is achieved only by knowing the truth.

Furthermore, we should not indulge in self-pity, dwell on the injustices of the past, or condemn or belittle ourselves; for to focus on these negatives makes it impossible to be delivered from these obstacles to spiritual unfoldment. Such ego qualities are transcended in the light of God, or in the knowledge that they have no power to enslave us if we do not identify with them.

The sense of ego, referred to as evil, is responsible for passion, anger, delusion, false desire, and unwillingness to accept God as the solution to our difficulties, miseries, and obstacles. It is important to remember that Jesus turned to God in all situations because he was conscious of God's inner guidance. He realized that only through God's grace could we be delivered from all evils.

The most important step in being delivered from evil is to know that we are incapable of doing it by ourselves. Every expression in the Lord's Prayer is directed to God as the

Father. *Thou* deliver us from evil. God alone can reveal to us our innate spirituality and freedom. We, however, must make the effort to receive God's guidance.

When Jesus prays for all humankind, he reveals a profound psychological and mystical truth regarding our innate nature. He recognizes the finitude of evil, the limitations of the ego, and the bondage of negative concepts and beliefs that envelop the world. Therefore, he could pray, "Deliver *us* from evil."

Furthermore, the Lord's Prayer reveals his profound compassion and love for suffering humanity. As a Bhakti yogi, his whole being flies toward God and takes all others with him. He recognizes that so long as one being is in bondage, his healing work is not complete. This recognition is based on the essential oneness of humankind, the Fatherhood and Divine Motherhood of God, and the interconnectedness of all human beings—the realization of unity in diversity, and duality in unity. Jesus furthermore reveals that freedom is the innate condition and birthright of every human being, whereas evil is a superimposition of ignorance on our spiritual nature, or Self-remembrance. To the degree that we attain individual freedom from evil, we also free others who are responsive to the ideal of spiritual liberation.

It is also evident in this prayer that Jesus reveals profound humility and spirituality by recognizing his oneness with all beings. He, too, had to transcend human imperfections, the delusions of the mind, and the dualities of life. He urged us not only to pray, but also to be vigilant at all times lest we succumb to the temptation of thinking ourselves above the delusions of the intellect and maneuvers of the ego. So long as we live in this world, temptation lies in wait for us.

What is temptation? The belief that one is separated from God. So long as the ego exists, the sense of separation appears real. This consciousness of a selfhood apart from God is characterized by the sense of "me and mine," the feeling of lack, the belief in personal power, the craving for personal possession, and the desire to dominate or control others.

What accounts for this appearance of evil when we accept the principle that everything is the manifestation of God? How can we hold God responsible for the existence of evil in this world? Since God is *not* the source of evil in any, then what is? For the answer to these questions, we have to look into our minds and hearts. The moment human vision became externalized and we perceived ourselves as entities existing in the world of duality, there arose a sense of separation in our minds. With this awakening to the world of duality, we lost sight of our true being, our spiritual unity, and our divine origin.

In the allegory of Adam and Eve in the Garden of Eden, the two lived at first in a state of natural felicity, harmony, and oneness, for they were completely rooted in God and at one with the Source of everything within and around them.

There was only pure Consciousness—the consciousness of bliss, purity, and love, appearing as all manifestations. What happened? None can fully comprehend. We only know that when humans became identified with the manifestations of God, they wanted to claim them for themselves. They no longer drew upon the Source, which until then had fully sustained them. In other words, they now permitted the sense of duality to become their reality, and the true Reality became a vague dream of a former idyllic existence.

The "fall of man," therefore, allegorizes the descent of consciousness into time and space. As we perceived the forms around us, our mind began to respond with desire to enjoy these forms, and with enjoyment came the desire to possess the forms and perpetuate the enjoyment. After extensive experience, we learn that the desire for enjoyment carries with it also the potential of pain. In religious terms, we call pleasure the "good," and pain the "evil." Continuous experience of pleasure and pain creates in us the belief that they are powers, since we pursue what is pleasurable and seek to escape from the painful. In our own mind, pain assumes the form of evil and pleasure the form of good. Thus for aeons humanity has been dominated by this dual belief in the power of good and evil. We have become the victims of our own dualistic thinking.

There are no sinners in the world, only expressions of ignorance that religions label "sins." The original nature of humankind always remains as pure as its Manifester.

However, forgetting our true nature, we, out of ignorance, commit "sins." As soon as we are born into this world, we automatically partake of the false beliefs and doctrines, superstitions and fears that dominate the world. False beliefs are like strong gusts of air that carry us along willy-nilly. These erroneous world beliefs insinuate themselves into our thinking at the subconscious level and are constantly reinforced at the conscious, thinking level, until the burden of limitation and negativity forces us to cry out for peace and freedom, for release from darkness and ignorance.

Only when we realize that we are the victims of false beliefs, values, impressions, and superstitions do we turn within and earnestly pray, *O God, deliver us from all these delusions, from this terrible sense of separation from Thee. Show us the way that leads from ignorance to enlightenment, from fear to understanding, from untruth to truth, from hatred to love, from darkness to light. Open our eyes that we may become aware of Thy light. Open our minds that we may become conscious of Thy truths. Open our hearts that we may feel Thy loving presence day and night. This is our unceasing prayer: Deliver us from evil by revealing to us that it is nonpower, that it is without law, power, and substance to sustain it, since it is not a part of Thee, O Lord of unity. Amen.*

Self-realized beings like Krishna, Buddha, Christ, and Shankara showed us how to free ourselves from the consciousness of evil. Shankara encouraged us to keep company with the virtuous; as he said, even a moment's association with a human being of Self-realization will furnish you with a boat to cross the sea of *samsara*, the world of relative existence and misery.

In the ancient scripture of India, the *Bhagavad-Gita*, Krishna, the Avatar, shows the path of Self-liberation to Arjuna, who stands for every devotee, so that finally Arjuna rejoices in his heart and exclaims, "Dispelled is my delusion. I have come to right remembrance...." [6] In other words, we can attain spiritual freedom from all temptations, or evils, even while living in the world.

Through the centuries we have sought to confront evil in different ways. Although we have struggled to overcome evil, evil persists. We have followed our own vengeful law—the old policy of an eye for an eye and a tooth for a tooth. The instinct for retribution still lingers in humankind and appears under various guises. Though we sense that we should live by the law of love, of spiritual nonviolence, we still act out the thought, "If someone hurts me, I'm going to strike back." Of course, society has reinforced this urge for revenge through repeated warfare on both communal and worldwide levels.

We still operate under the impulse of fighting evil with evil, although the saviors have repeatedly reminded us that evil can never be abolished by counter-evil, that violence is never overcome by violence. Gautama, the Enlightened One, taught: "Hatred is never conquered by hatred, nor enmity by enmity. But by making himself subjectively free from [these] feelings…one can most surely conquer these. This is truth and the eternal law." [7]

The same truth was reaffirmed some 500 years later by Jesus the Christ in these arresting words: "Resist not evil." "Love your enemies, bless them that curse you, do good to them that hate you, and pray for them that despitefully use you and persecute you; that ye might be the children of your Father which is in heaven." [8]

Until we realize this truth for ourselves and apply it in every area of life, we will be dominated by evil, by hatred, by sorrow, and by misery. The mystic is not impressed by followers who broadcast their love for their savior and yet manifest hatred toward those who do not accept their savior or avatar as the only one to be worshiped. How inconsistent this negative, hostile, unloving attitude is with the teachings of these Avatars, such as Krishna, Buddha, and Christ!

Let us benefit by the wisdom and love of the avatars and keep company with the enlightened ones in our minds and hearts. Thus we can free ourselves from the evils or delusions of the worldly minded and the ignorant.

How else can we learn to rise above the negativity of the ego? Swami Shankara, the founder of the ancient Swami Order in India in the 8th century A.D., taught us: "If thou desirest peace and emancipation, learn to be equally loving and kind to all. There is but one Reality that permeates thee and me, and all beings. Then why dost thou lose thy forbearance and become angry? Rise above the consciousness of separation and realize thyself in all and all in thee." [9]

Krishna also instructs Arjuna to transcend the consciousness of evil by subjectively rising above the pairs of opposites—such as pleasure and pain, gain and loss, victory and defeat, praise and blame—by dedicating all actions, thoughts, and desires to God, and by performing all works in the love and consciousness of God. Thus we free ourselves from the tyranny of the ego, since it has no existence in God-consciousness.

The temptations of humankind have no ultimate reality for they are only appearances. No matter how real, continuous, and persistent they appear to be, they are nonetheless finite and insubstantial. If it were not so, temptations could never be overcome.

Not only must we uproot temptation but we must also transcend ego-consciousness, the *root* of all temptations. In the Lord's Prayer, Jesus reveals to us that we must transcend the ego sense itself; for only in self-transcendence are all temptations—children of the ego—overcome. When we realize freedom from the ego's control, we regain the conscious awareness of our spiritual identity and perfection.

Where is this ego to be transcended? The Master of Galilee showed that only within a human being's own self can it be overcome. The evidence that we are freeing ourselves from the bondage of the sensory self is that we stop reacting to the fears, superstitions, and prejudices of the worldly minded. In the measure that we no longer react negatively to any condition, circumstance, or person, we have become delivered from the tyranny of the diabolic ego.

By the power of love we transcend all negativity, as Jesus demonstrated in his encounter with Mary of Magdala and her vindictive accusers. They scornfully flung her at his feet with the intent of gaining his support for their condemnation of her adultery. In their blinded vision, they had already sentenced her to be stoned. Jesus, however, recognized their impure motive and flagrant self-righteousness. Therefore, he turned to the crowd, masterfully saying, "He that is without sin among you, let him first cast a stone at her." [10] Slowly, her accusers departed one by one. Only Mary of Magdala remained. With eyes full of compassion and understanding, he raised her from the ground and assured her with words of wisdom, "Neither do I condemn thee: go, and sin no more." [11] Jesus perceived her potential saintliness and responded with love and compassion.

Another example that shows Jesus' transcendence of the ego through the expression of divine compassion is revealed in his encounter with Peter who had thrice denied him. As Jesus passed through the outer court and saw Peter, Jesus simply turned to look lovingly at him without a word of retribution or reproach. Peter realized that he had failed to live up to his earlier claim that he would never fail or deny his Master. Feeling his Master's profound compassion, love, and understanding, Peter could not bear the impact of his guru's penetrating gaze. Jesus neither condemned nor judged, for he perceived that Peter acted out of fear and weakness. Such is the transforming power of love that Peter's whole life was changed from one of spiritual cowardice to fearlessness and sublime self-dedication to his Master's work.

Another evidence of Christ's transcendence of ego-consciousness is revealed in Judas' betrayal of him. When Jesus saw Judas approaching with the Roman soldiers to arrest him in the Garden of Gethsemane, Jesus addressed him as *friend*: "Friend, wherefore art thou come?" [12] Had Jesus been dominated by ego-consciousness, he would have reacted bitterly and reproached him for his betrayal.

Suppose another deceives you. What is your reaction? Do you reproach that one, or do you rise above the situation and sincerely pray, "Infinite Love, forgive that being for acting in ignorance"? Of course, the one who acted harmfully to you may think those actions were committed very knowingly. But one who deceives another or acts out of cruelty cannot really act knowingly, since such actions are not being guided by the light of truth. Such a person is dominated by the force of ignorance and egotism.

Again, at the moment of crucifixion, Jesus projected the quintessential power of love and forgiveness over the negativity of the ego. It is difficult enough to respond with love, forgiveness, and understanding to even one person who has injured us; but when we are asked to forgive any number of people who have hurt us, we consider that to be beyond our capacity, and we invent various reasons for not forgiving them.

The principle of forgiveness is the same, whether we are dealing with one or a hundred people. We have to look beyond the injury or injustice to the indwelling Presence, the Divine within us, and fervently pray, "Father, Mother, Beloved, Friend, forgive them, for they are in a state of ignorance, which blinds them to the love and power of soul." Only those who have transcended evil within themselves can look out at the unrighteous, the cruel, and the unjust, and sincerely respond with their soul, praying, "Father, forgive them, for they know not what they do."

Thus, one of the most practical means of overcoming sensory bondage and the appearances of negativity is to look *beyond* the appearances, beyond the form, beyond the individual, to the indwelling Presence and contemplate this divine Presence in all its fullness.

The Lord's Prayer points to the truth that we must not judge according to appearances. As Jesus repeatedly stressed in his teaching, "Judge not, that ye be not judged. For with what judgment ye judge, ye shall be judged: and with what measure ye mete, it shall be measured to you again." [13]

Rather than to judge another, we need to perceive the Real in the midst of the phenomenal. Right judgment is discerning every being as God individualized; it is learning to love every being as our own Self. When we love our own Self as a child of God and see others as children of God, we will love one another as equals, even as God the Divine Parent loves us all equally. Indeed, "Thou shalt love thy neighbor as thyself." [14] When we are pervaded with such unconditional love, we will love everyone as the manifestation of the same Reality. Then it is possible to pray for our enemies with a forgiving heart because we know that we have no enemies when love pervades our consciousness. In loving divinely, we experience awareness of our spiritual oneness. Let us remember that in God there is no separation and distinction, only the eternal bond of loving oneness and spiritual Self-expression.

To pray for one's enemy is to offer prayer to one's own Self. How, exactly, is this achieved? When we fill our consciousness with the remembrances of God and God's qualities, our heart becomes pure. A pure heart can no longer attract or contain impure thoughts. Therefore, the thought of an enemy no longer exists in the pure heart. Whatever negative impression may arise with regard to anyone is immediately dismissed by reestablishing one's mind on the spiritual nature and identity of the Self. In the presence of God-consciousness, the thought of an enemy cannot arise, because "I and my Father are one," "I and my Divine Mother are one."

In praying for another we bless ourselves and recognize our
spiritual kinship and identity with others. Whatever thoughts
we entertain about another invariably reach the one toward
whom they are directed and continue to affect and influence
our own life.

If we have the consciousness that anyone is our enemy,
we have need to pray. Therefore, let our prayer be:
O God, our Beloved, who art the creative power, infinite love,
and ocean of mercy, fill my mind with such purity and love that
no unrighteousness may enter my consciousness. Grant that I
may love all as Thou lovest me. Inspire me to perceive only
Thy glory in those who are living in ignorance and misery,
hatred and hostility, so that they may be awakened to their
true spiritual glory, the one Self abiding in all.

When the Lord's Prayer is sincerely and seriously offered,
it delivers us from the consciousness of cruelty, impurity,
and selfishness. Let us never forget that as finite human
beings we cannot free ourselves from enmity or hatred;
but by the power of God's love and wisdom within us, we
surely can become free from these destructive emotions.

Furthermore, to forgive our enemies requires us to stop
judging them according to our own limited understanding,
prejudices, and ignorance. Whatever thought we entertain
about another reveals what we think of ourselves; that is,
by judging others, we are passing judgment on ourselves.
To compare one's self with another from the standpoint of

the ego is to render a disservice to one's self and others.

What is true judgment, when applied to the practice of forgiveness? "Judge not according to the appearance, but judge righteous judgment." [15] To judge righteously is to perceive Reality in the midst of the phenomenal, the truth amidst falsehood, the changeless in change, the infinite beyond the finite, the pure beyond the impure, the Self behind the nonself. We judge righteously by loving everyone, acknowledging the presence of God in them, invoking their spiritual attributes, and guiding them through personal spiritual unfoldment to manifest their own innate perfection.

To love one's Self is the basis of forgiveness. This love is not conditioned by the ego or the senses, by self-interest or impure motive; it is the natural expression of God in humankind, which is Love itself. When you can honestly say, "I feel that we are all one," then it is possible to love all others in that oneness. We cannot forgive another so long as we cling to our misconceptions, false beliefs, prejudices, ignorance, and, above all, to our obdurate position of separateness between ourselves and others.

We cannot forgive another if we are unwilling to concede the possibility that we ourselves are capable of error. Nor do our words of forgiveness have any meaning so long as we still harbor the self-righteous attitude that we are superior to another, that we are forgiving the other. Only Soul can offer forgiveness, because Soul functions in the consciousness of spiritual oneness.

Another important principle of forgiveness that Jesus forcefully reveals in his prayer is that evil *per se* is not an eternal reality or power. If it were, deliverance from evil would be impossible.

The Lord's Prayer furthermore reveals that only by contacting the pure, transcendent God-consciousness can It free humankind from the clutches of evil. Only by acknowledging the divine Presence as the sole power can It work through us to free us from our false beliefs and fears. Jesus prayed for deliverance from evil because he realized that evil is not overcome by resisting, suppressing, or ignoring it. He taught us, "Resist not evil." [16]

What is the psychology of nonresistance to evil? It is the recognition that evil is a state of self-delusion. Evil is our subjective concept; and since it is not of God, it has no substance, law, or power to support it. By resisting evil, on the other hand, we impute to it a power or reality, which then acts according to our belief. Resistance, in other words, gives temporal or mental power to the object of resistance. When we fully know the truth of evil as an appearance, our mind is freed from its influence.

By recognizing God as Love and Law, the only Power and Cause, the mesmerism of the world—its dualistic beliefs, superstitions, and fear—is shattered. Love is the only power that dissolves the sense of duality, feelings of conflict, and states of confusion. If we are to know peace in fellowship, peace in the world, peace in our hearts, we have to keep our minds upon the divine Reality and eternal truths.

In praying for freedom from evil, we must also be prepared to transcend good, since we cannot transcend one without the other. Both good and evil exist as interrelated concepts, like two sides of a coin. Only spiritual perfection transcends the concept of good and evil. In Self-transcendence, absolute freedom is realized.

Thus Christ gave us the inner assurance, born of his Self-illumination and attainment of unconditional freedom in transcendental perfection, that every being—no matter how deluded, unrighteous, or dominated by impurities—has the potential to transform, transmute, and transcend all negativeness, all feelings of limitation, and all conditions of imperfection. Jesus came to reveal to us how to attain spiritual freedom even while living in this world. In the Lord's Prayer he has shown the way that is open to every being.

Thine Is the Kingdom, and the Power, and the Glory, Forever. Amen

Meditation

Beloved ones—and I use that term advisedly, for we are the beloveds of God—God loves us whether we know God and love God as our own Self; but only when our heart turns in devotion toward God do we become aware of God's boundless love for us.

Even though we give many names to God, no name can express the depth of our love for the Divine; nor can any name contain the nature of God or the love of God. Humankind has an innate need to be devoted to That for which name and form are only external symbols. That Reality beyond name and form is known by the code word God, or Aum.

Among the many names humankind gives to God is the name Krishna. Krishna signifies "the one who attracts or draws the whole universe unto himself," or, "the one to whom the whole universe is attracted." And what can be more attracting, or more attractive, than the power of Love, which is God, or Krishna? Love is the universal, all-pervading, attracting power.

We know that the power of love is real, for it alone can bestow lasting joy, peace, and freedom. It alone is real and paramount in life, for none can live without it. We seek to express love in infinite ways. With spiritual unfoldment, we realize that all beings and creatures are dear to us because of the real love that shines through them. This love is unlimited, because it cannot be contained by any form, and it can never be fully expressed by any being. By the power of love we can transform all our experiences into spiritual expressions. When we identify our body, mind, heart, and soul with the ideal of loving oneness, then the beloved One can manifest through us and reveal the blissfulness and purity of infinite Love.

How do we attain the consciousness of God's love? By offering prayer and meditation with a devout heart to the indwelling Presence. When we daily meditate, contemplate, and remember the nature of God, we become firmly established in the consciousness of God's love. Meditation is the conscious awareness and recognition that God alone constitutes the power, the glory, and the perfection of our life.

When we behold the nature and attributes of God within us, our vision expands to embrace all life in the consciousness of reverence and love. It is integral to meditation to perceive the glory of God in and through God's creation—God's expression, God's projection—but it is even more important to remember that God is also beyond God's manifestation. No matter how magnificent the creation may be, no matter how much pleasure we take in name and form, there can be no spiritual fulfillment and freedom unless we realize that the Source is our own Self, and that all creations exist within that Self.

The Self is God, the all-pervading Reality of absolute existence, creative intelligence, and all-sustaining power. It is Self-contained, and contains all within Itself. When we realize this truth in meditation, we remain content within ourselves.

The true yogi lives in the consciousness of inner unity and outer harmony. A yogi is truly spiritual who no longer beholds any separation between oneself and God and the universe. To grow spiritually, we have to express our awareness of truth through all activities and relationships. Until we do this, we are simply indulging in mental gymnastics, intellectual play, and sensory gratification.

Meditation is that holy, subjective communion within the

sanctum sanctorum, the Holy of Holies, wherein the individual self merges within Itself. In meditation we come upon this Reality that is free from mutation, from time, name, and form. So long as our awareness remains limited to the mind, we want to preserve the impermanent, such as our body, possessions, and human relationships; but when we discover that we are essentially the changeless Reality, we can accept the changes of birth and death with equanimity and wisdom. Such is the fruit of meditation.

How can we know that there is a changeless Reality within ourselves? This knowledge is gained by making the following observation: You are aware of change. In order to be aware of any object, there has to be Self-consciousness, or Self-awareness. The consciousness that observes change is the eternal Witness. Whatever is known is possible because of the omniscient Self. The changeless Self is immortal, indestructible, and infinite. When we realize ourselves as the Self, we know that everything arises, exists, and merges in the Self. Thus we understand that first there is the recognition, "I am the individual self, endowed with the faculty to perceive the activities and manifestations of my true Self."

You are aware of yourself as an individual, are you not? Where was that awareness when you were a child? Always within you. It is this selfsame awareness that preserves the memories of all your experiences and of every stage of growth. It is not possible to have all these memories and recollections unless there is a unitive, synthesizing, changeless consciousness underlying all impressions and changes.

Observe for a moment what happens when you are aware of changes. Where do these changes take place? In the mind, the instrument of perception. The mind is shaped and influenced by its perceptions of change, but the Self, which is pure consciousness, remains the changeless Witness of the mind and its activities.

Let us consider the example of the film and the movie screen. The images are in the film, not in the screen. However, if we did not know this, we would think that the images were in the screen. Yet no matter what happens in the film, the screen remains unaffected and unchanged. In other words, the changes take place in the film, or the mind, but not in the Self, or the Self-consciousness. The Self is the Perceiver, the Witness, beyond form, beyond change, beyond birth and death. Therefore, it is called the Real, or the ultimate Reality.

When we comprehend this truth, all human experiences are perceived as dream images that need not disturb, frighten, or delude us. What freedom and joy are awakened and sustained in us by this knowledge gathered in meditation: Our real nature or Self is eternally free from self-limitations, from injury, pain, fear, and death—from all finiteness, mental or physical.

Although we may intellectually accept the idea of the

changeless Self behind all changes, it does not liberate
us until it has become an inner realization. When we are
consciously aware of this truth, we no longer find ourselves
reacting negatively or blindly toward the world. Guided
by an understanding heart, we remain at peace. With
understanding comes freedom from misinterpreting the
nature of the world and humankind. In fact, we no longer
judge according to appearances, and we no longer condemn
anyone for their failings. Instead, we understand and
love unconditionally.

With the awakening of spiritual understanding and
impartial love, our mind acquires a positive and constructive
orientation. Such a mind is no longer restless but full of
clarity and peace. No longer dominated by the world's
flutterings or vanities, we are free to know the truth:
We are the eternal Self, ever free and changeless, full of
love and good will, peace and truth.

The Lord's Prayer can guide us back to this awareness of
spiritual freedom and perfection. It can help us discard
all our self-limitations, the sense of estrangement from
others, and conflict with the world. Have you worked
with the principle, "Our Father"? In relationships with
our fellow beings of diverse religious persuasions, nationality,
or race, do we remember that our Father is also their Father,
our Divine Mother is also their Divine Mother? Then
there is only one spiritual relationship for us all. We are
all equally the sons and daughters of God; therefore we

are all brothers and sisters. If we perceive this truth in our hearts, then all our animosities and prejudices will disappear.

Every time we call another a sinner, every time we judge and condemn, we are praying amiss; that is, we are forgetting that we are all one and that we have a spiritual responsibility to express our oneness. Through the Lord's Prayer we can come to a fuller recognition of our capacity to receive and share God's love and wisdom with the whole universe.

To grow in understanding of this prayer, we need to offer each word repeatedly, sacredly, and meditatively. If we remain faithful to this prayer, we will be blessed with the awareness of the Father within us, the Mother within us, and that we are one with that Divinity. Jesus of Christ-consciousness reminded us of our spiritual heritage when he said, "I and my Father are one." The whole prayer is an expression and acknowledgment of spiritual oneness, which each of us can come to realize.

Unless the Lord's Prayer is offered with our whole being turned toward God, it is of no value to us. In fact, it is a sacrilege to give it merely lip service, uttering it unthinkingly, unfeelingly and in such haste as though we were pressed for time or afraid of missing something more important in the world.

It is helpful to remember the importance of this prayer in the life of Christ. Whenever you are tempted to recite the prayer in a hurry, stop for a moment to ask yourself, how did Jesus offer this prayer—in haste, or patiently, reverently, and lovingly? The more we repeat the Lord's Prayer with profound devotion and reflection, the more it will express our inner nature and reflect our spiritual understanding.

Thine Is the Kingdom

When we pray, "O Father, Thine is the kingdom," can we sense or intuit what Christ sought to project through these words—how deeply he felt the significance of this world being the world of God?

The spiritual significance of this expression, "Thine is the kingdom, and the power, and the glory," is the supreme lesson of nonattachment. Most human thinking revolves around our desires and attachments. Whenever we become attached to any person or any thing, we feel the desire to possess, dominate, control, and manipulate it. We also fear the loss of our possessions. When we reflect on our life we invariably discover that all our sufferings result not from any external cause, but from our personal attachments to others or to things, to ideas, beliefs, and structures. This is the malaise of our society.

Even when we say that we love someone, do we not really mean we are attached to another? Perfect love is free from all attachment and the desire to possess and control. Every time we use the expressions "me and mine," and "you and yours," we are reinforcing our sense of attachment. Attachment breeds fear, and it corrupts the purity of thought and love of heart.

When we are attached, we experience pain arising from the fear of separation from our attachment. We cling to our images. When we discover that they are shattered like the window pane, we grow disillusioned, disheartened, and cynical. We experience much suffering before we free ourselves from attachment. Every image of attachment has to be shattered before the pure Spirit can manifest.

Is it not curious that all the saviors have emphasized the importance of nonattachment in life? Christ says renounce all thou hast, and follow me. That is, we are to renounce the consciousness of attachment by following the saving Truth that is always accessible to us, since it is the core of our existence, the source of our being, and the liberator of our mind from the thralldom of sensory enslavement.

Shankarachariya, the founder of the ancient Swami Order of India, declares, "Beware! The adder of sense-attachment has struck humanity and the whole world is infused with the venom of misery." [1]

Buddha reflected on the sorrows that arise from sensory attachment and urged us to free ourselves by self-transcendence. He taught that we alone are the friend of ourselves, as well as our own worst enemy. By recognizing that the Self alone is the fulfillment of all true aspirations and needs, we gradually cease to become personally attached to any being. Personal attachment invariably brings suffering, yet this very suffering awakens in us the resolve to free ourselves from it. We cannot serve God and mammon, meaning God-consciousness and worldly mindedness.

There is no joy until we renounce our sensory attachments and mental bondage to our self-limiting concepts about ourselves, about others, and about our world. There is only joy when we consciously connect with the current of joy that resides in the depth of our being. It requires tremendous inner strength and willingness to examine impartially one's attachments and obsessions and to admit that these indeed are responsible for one's sufferings.

After experiencing pain and disillusionment in one human relationship, how often we delude ourselves by forming new personal attachments, thinking that this time it will somehow be a lasting, ideal relationship. It never happens. The very nature of selfishness denies the spirit of unity and perfection; it ignores the truth, or is ignorant of the nature of truth. There can only be freedom in unity, never in attachments, which are a disturbance of the unity itself; that is, they are a deviation from the Real.

Why do we refuse to recognize the truth regarding our personal attachments? Why do we insist on clinging to the finite, mentally claiming everything that comes within our purview as our own? Why do we not examine the content of our mind? Because we fear to expose ourselves, our weaknesses and inadequacies. Self-exposure invariably brings pain before it brings relief, and we do not know how to cope with our anguish. Furthermore, we fear exposing ourselves to others because we wish to preserve a flattering self-image. We are also aware that others have a fixed image of us, which we are expected to maintain to have their acceptance and approval. So long as we remain self-imprisoned, a slave to our possessions and deluded intellect, we will never know the truth about our glorious Self, and we will never be free to be ourselves.

If we impartially reflect on the pain that arises from personal attachment, we realize that all our sufferings are rooted in attachment. This realization brings a degree of Self-liberation; we suddenly know with inmost certainty that we have the capacity to be free, to shatter any image of self-delusion and self-deception. We know that we do not have to live up to someone else's image of ourselves, for this is simply catering to egotism and delusion.

Every time we are tempted to claim anything for ourselves, it will be helpful to remember, "Thine is the kingdom." In this expanded recognition, we discover that our well-being, our highest good, and our true needs are not diminished, but realized. Nonattachment as expressed in Jesus' words, "Thine is the kingdom," also bears witness to the truth that only through complete reliance on the Father within—the Divine Mother, the creative image maker—can we live honestly and with spiritual integrity.

To pray "Thine is the kingdom" implies no sense of lack, but acknowledges the divine Source within us in Its infinite abundance. It is the prayer of one who knows that the Infinite is the only creative, all-sustaining power in the universe, that everything belongs to the Infinite since it is the manifestation of Its love, power, wisdom, law, and life.

This prayer, "Thine is the kingdom," also reflects the devotee's recognition that the nature of God is the infinite Reality, which is teeming with all the ideas, inspiration, substance, and guidance that we need for our sustenance and self-expression.

Another truth revealed in this expression is that we can call nothing our own, that we have nothing of our own, and are nothing on our own, but by the grace of God we have access to everything that is of God. As the Christ reminds us, "All that the Father has is thine," because we all are God's beloved expressions. Therefore, how can we ever truly lack for anything to lead a life of joyous fulfillment?

Furthermore, when we acknowledge that this whole cosmic manifestation belongs to God, we unfold an inner freedom in which there is no longer any consciousness of being burdened or dominated by the things of this world. When we can awaken each day with the recognition that "Thine is the kingdom," it removes our fear of believing that we have to enslave, deceive, or manipulate anyone to fulfill our needs. When we acknowledge that "Thine is the kingdom," our minds are receptive to the spontaneous flow of God's treasures into objective expression in our life.

What a sublime state of consciousness to know with absolute inner conviction and to feel with our whole being that everything is Thine, the ever present and active Source of fulfillment! How enthralling to be free from the consciousness of possession and personal attachment, to be liberated from the delusive ego-sense, to be free to enjoy all the things we have in the consciousness that all is "Thine." *As we strive to attain the state of consciousness wherein everything is Thine, O Lord, we are inspired to dedicate ourselves and use our possessions in Thy service.* No one who realizes that "Thine is the kingdom" ever feels destitute, lonely, deprived, or any sense of lack. When we know that "Thine is the kingdom," we are keeping the channel open for Thy kingdom to express itself abundantly through us to the world.

"Thine is the kingdom" encompasses body, mind, heart and soul—everything that exists. It is all Thine, no longer mine. Gone, gone forever, is the consciousness of possession and attachment. Dissolved is the distinction between "mine" and "Thine." Now there is only Thine, and even when I say "mine," it means but Thine.

In this expression, "Thine is the kingdom," Jesus once again reveals his complete humility and total acceptance of God as the sole Provider. Humility is profound spiritual strength. It is the recognition that everything belongs to God and has come from God. It is the awareness of one's relationship to God, the individual to the universal, the manifest to the unmanifest, the lesser to the greater, and the many to the One.

The humble heart stands in awe of this infinite Reality, the all-loving God who is so vast, transcendental, and all-pervading, so inexhaustible in pure love and resources, that God can provide, sustain, and nourish all God's expressions without experiencing any loss or limitation.

To be aware of God as the infinite Consciousness within us fills us with joyous humility and freedom of soul. Only the free soul can live by this truth, that "Thine is the kingdom." Negative qualities, such as arrogance, vanity, and pride are expressions of spiritual cowardice, moral weakness, and lack of Self-awareness. A child of God is not dominated by the consciousness of egotism but is sustained and inspired by the spirit of selfless devotion. A child of God is unencumbered by the sense of separation from the all-sustaining and all-governing Source. A devotee who offers this prayer, "Thine is the kingdom," surrenders his or her self completely to God.

What is self-surrender? Self-surrender is the innate expression of true humility. It is one's complete identification with God. It is merging one's self in the cosmic Self. It is accepting the greater for the lesser, the infinite for the finite, the glory of God for the paltry, insubstantial, vainglorious things of the world. Self-surrender is complete identification in body, mind, heart, and soul with the Infinite.

What an inspired conclusion to the Lord's prayer is the thought, "Thine is the kingdom." It is like a beautiful symphony that begins with the full orchestra playing together the theme "Our Father," and melting together into the expression of praise and joyous self-surrender, culminating exuberantly in "Thine is the kingdom." The spirit of self-surrender fills us to overflowing with feelings of thanksgiving and peace.

For example, when you view a glorious sunset you feel an inner contentment arise in you. In that perception of beauty there is no attachment, no desire to dominate or to possess or to change anything. There is only the freedom of witnessing a manifestation of God's kingdom. It is only when we are dominated by personal desire that we lose touch with our true Self with all Its vastness, joy, and beauty.

Can we enjoy Thy kingdom, O God, and the things of this world without possessive consciousness? Surely our limitations and sufferings do not arise on account of our possessions, since all are Thy manifestations; but it is the consciousness of possession that looks at things and declares, "See, all this is mine! Look at all I have!" These feelings of possessiveness extend not only to one's belongings or family, but to one's country or nationality. What has happened to all human conquests—the mighty, ancient empires of Darius and Alexander, the Caesars, Charlemagne and the Hapsburgs?

Where is human glory? Where are the emperors, kings and princes, dictators and presidents, who sought to wrest the kingdom from God and make it their own? They have all perished. Their empires lie buried beneath the desert sands and oceans. The ancient civilizations in all their glory are but a distant memory, all bearing witness to the evanescence of temporal achievements and vainglorious victories.

When we forget that God is the King, we quickly substitute ourselves as the king of Thy kingdom. In fact, many a king has sought to immortalize and deify himself by having monuments erected to his name and glory.

One such self-deluded king passed an edict in his kingdom that he alone was to be worshiped as the official god. Anyone who refused to obey this decree would find release through immediate death. The king had a son who was deeply spiritual and acknowledged only the supreme Reality, the divine Creator—God as love and as worthy of worship.

The first word he spoke was the name of God. When the king discovered his son singing praises to God, he took him aside and angrily reminded him that *he* was god, and he alone was to be worshiped. His son, however, continued singing the praises of God.

Then his father threatened him. "Don't you know that I can have you killed for violating my edict and refusing to worship me alone as your god? If you want to praise God, sing my praises, for I am your god."

The son, however, refused to bow to his father's pretension to power. His father had him incarcerated, but this only encouraged the son to keep praising Lord Krishna all the more fervently.

The king devised various cruel tortures to convert his son, but the son could not be frightened by his father's cruelty. The son declared, "God will protect me, God will take care of me." The king reminded his son that the whole world feared the king and his power—even the gods scattered in fear when the king came on the scene.

During one of his journeys, the king sought out Vishnu, the Lord of Love; but he could not find him. The deluded king thought that the Lord of Love had disappeared due to fear of the king. When Vishnu was asked about this, he said, "Well, it is indeed true that the evil king could not find me anywhere, but that was because I concealed myself in his heart."

"Why could he not find you in his heart, O Vishnu?" asked a saint.

The Lord of Love answered, "Because he would not bend his head."

Indeed, the kingdom of God is within us, but we will never know this unless we bend our heads, that is, bow down in our minds and hearts at the altar of God within us. As Krishna proclaims in the *Gita*, "I dwell in all hearts."

Thine Is the Power

Power has three aspects: the creative power, the preserving power, and the transforming power. Remember when Pontius Pilate, with all the might and power of the Roman Empire behind him, threatened Jesus? When Jesus was brought before him, Pilate asked him, "Don't you know I have power over your life and death? I can kill you if I so choose."

What was Jesus' reaction to this threat? He spoke with the authority of Self-knowledge and spiritual courage, "Thou couldest have no power at all against me, except it were given thee from above." [2]

There is no other power in heaven or earth save the power

of God. Every time we forget that truth, we become dominated by fear in its various forms, such as fear of personal injury, deprivation, or disaster. All our fears arise from this false perception, or belief in two powers: the power of God and a power opposed to God.

There is only one power, but each of us uses that power either for selfish or unselfish purposes. When, however, we finally realize that God is the one all-pervading power, we use it for unselfish and constructive purposes. We cannot help but express God's love and beauty when we truly know that "Thine is the power."

Thine Is the Glory

What is the glory of God? It is transcendental, beyond expression. It is also all-pervading, yet made manifest in this world.

In the *Gita*, the scripture of yoga and the science of Brahman, Krishna the Avatar teaches, "Whatever is glorious, beautiful, or good and powerful in the universe of creation, know that to be the manifestation of but a portion of my splendor." [3]

When Moses longs to behold the glory of God, God reveals only a ray of His glory, for if Moses were to see God in His full glory he would be blinded by this vision and surely die.

What is the divine glory? The glory of God is God's goodness, beauty, love, and perfection in creation and in humankind. Why do we sometimes perceive the glory of this creation and respond to it with feelings of wonder, joy, and love? Or why do we respond to the smile of a child? Because we are, consciously or intuitively, recognizing these as the expressions of God's glory.

When you look within to behold the light of God, this is a manifestation of God's glory. And when you feel the transforming power of love in your life, this, too, is the glory of God.

How can we meditate on the glory of God in creation? By contemplating the attributes or nature of God—God's creative power, guiding intelligence, manifestations of beauty, and embodiments of love. These attributes are inherent in creation; otherwise Christ could not have made his observation of the lily in the field and reflected that even Solomon in all his glory was not arrayed like one of these.

Whatever you call beautiful, lovely, good, gentle; or wherever you behold expressions of kindliness, understanding, purity, and selflessness, you are bearing witness to the glories of God. Is there any object or being who does not reflect to some measure the glory of God? The more we contemplate the spiritual nature of humankind, the greater becomes our

joy and surprise in perceiving God's glory. Behind our love
of any form is God, the all-beautiful, all-perfect, and all-
loving Presence.

You may meditate on God in the form, or meditate on the
form in God. Whatever is glorious is eternal, infinite, and
pure. It admits of no limitation, imperfection, or finitude.
One who recognizes that "Thine is the glory" offers all
actions and their fruits to God. The devotee of God seeks no
personal glory, no self-aggrandizement, no praise, no flattery,
no favoritism. A devotee's constant joy is in perceiving God
everywhere and in everyone. A devotee is not deluded by
human claims of personal power, possessions, and honors.
A devotee is at peace, knowing that everything is the
manifestation of God and that God is the source and provider
for all earthly needs. And finally a devotee realizes with
appreciative heart and pure mind that there is no life,
no sustenance, no wisdom, no peace, and no joy apart from
life in God, the one and only Love.

Amen

"Amen" expresses the recognition that this prayer is to
be fulfilled in our life of service, meditation, and Self-
unfoldment. It reminds us that we are receptive to God's
guidance. We have now entered the inner silence, which is
beyond speech, beyond human thought, beyond personal
desires, and free from all impure motives. Now the devotee

listens with inner attentiveness to receive God's guidance and instruction, to fulfill God's will, to manifest God's glory and express God's perfection in all aspects of life. The amen is an expression of inner trust and complete assurance that God's will is being fulfilled. Therefore, so be it.

Peace be with you.

Thine is the Kingdom, and the Power, and the Glory, Forever

Endnotes

Introduction: Jesus the Christ, a Yogi

1. Matthew: 11:29, 30 *(All Bible references are from the King James Version.)*
2. *Bhagavad-Gita*, II, 55, translation by Swami Premananda
3. John 15:12
4. *Bhagavad-Gita*, VII, 16, 17
5. *Yoga Sutras*, 3-2
6. F. Max Müller, *Ramakrishna – His Life and Sayings*, p. 111
7. John 14:20
8. *Bhagavad-Gita*, V, 24
9. *Bhagavad-Gita*, IV, 20-22
10. John 5:19
11. John 5:30
12. John 13:14
13. *Bhagavad-Gita*, II, 48

Our Father, Which Art in Heaven, Hallowed Be Thy Name

1. Exodus 3:14
2. John 8:58
3. *Bhagavad-Gita*, IX, 11
4. *Rig Veda 1*. 164, 46
5. John 10:30

6. Matthew 6:9
7. Luke 2:49
8. Luke 23:34
9. Luke 23:46
10. Luke 4:8
11. 1 John 1:5
12. John 8:32
13. Matthew 7:7
14. Luke 17:21
15. Matthew 5:48
16. John 16:23
17. John 1:1
18. Romans 8:28
19. Swami Prabhavananda,
    The Spiritual Heritage of India,
    p. 331
20. Proverbs 18:10

Thy Kingdom Come, Thy Will Be Done in Earth as It Is in Heaven

1. Matthew 12:48, 50
2. Luke 23:34
3. John 15:11
4. Genesis 1:27
5. *Dhammapada*, X, 129
6. Proverbs 23:7

Give Us This Day Our Daily Bread

1. Galatians 6:7
2. Matthew 7:2
3. John 12:32
4. John 4:24
5. *Bhagavad-Gita*, IV, 11
6. John 14:6
7. Matthew 7:7
8. Matthew 5:6
9. Matthew 5:16
10. *Dhammapada*, XV, II
11. Matthew 6:32
12. Mark 11:24
13. John 6: 48-51
14. John 6: 32, 33
15. *Bhagavad-Gita*, IV, 24
16. Matthew 5:6

Forgive Us Our Debts as We Forgive Our Debtors

1. Acts 17:25
2. Revelation 3:20
3. John 16:33
4. John 17:15
5. Matthew 5:48
6. Psalm 46:10
7. *Svetasvatara Upanishad*: II, 5
8. Matthew 27:46

9. John 8:11
10. *Chandogya Upanishad:* III,
Part 14, verse 1
11. Matthew 5:44

Let Us Not Enter into Temptation

1. Isaiah 26:3
2. Proverbs 23:7
3. Ancient Vedic prayer of Self-realization
4. James 1:13
5. Matthew 4:4
6. Mark 8:36
7. Exodus 20:3
8. Luke 4:8

Deliver Us from Evil

1. Matthew 5:48
2. Matthew 13:31, 32
3. Matthew 13:45, 46
4. Matthew 13:47, 48.
   a. See also: Matthew 13:33, 34;
   Matthew 18:23-35; Matthew 20:1-16;
   Matthew 22:2-14, 25; Matthew 25:1-13,
   14-30
5. *Bhagavad-Gita*, II, 16
6. *Bhagavad-Gita*, XVIII, 73
7. *Dhammapada*, I, 5

8. Matthew 5:44-45
9. *Moha-Mudgar*, Verses 13, 14
10. John 8:7
11. John 8:11
12. Matthew 26:50
13. Matthew 7:1, 2
14. Matthew 19:19
15. John 7:24
16. Matthew 5:39

Thine Is the Kingdom, and the Power, and the Glory, Forever. Amen

1. *Moha-Mudgar*, Verse 3
2. John 19:11
3. *Bhagavad-Gita*, X, 41

Acknowledgments

Heartfelt thanks to Srimati Shanti Mataji (Carolyn Hatt) and Einar Raysor, who provided editorial assistance for an earlier version of this book. Their clarity of vision and love of Soul is present in this version, too. We honor them for helping form a precious spiritual path for all to walk upon.

Blessings and gratitude to Shraddha, Padma, Shambhu, and Anna Landewe, for being part of an amazing team that brings you the book in its present form. Their dedication and talent in bringing beauty and truth into visibility are profound and moving.

Joyful appreciation for Arietta, Beverly Diaz, Karuna, Lakshmi, and Virginia Vaughn, who provided proofreading for this version. Their devotion and grace infuse every page, and we are grateful!

About the Author

Sri Swami Shankarananda (1935–2014) was a Western yogi and an illumined master teaching the universal truth of Vedanta in Baltimore, Maryland, where he established the Divine Life Church of Absolute Oneness. He was a guru, of the line of gurus that began with Babaji. His grandfather guru (Paramguru) was Swami Yogananda Paramhansa, author of the classic book *Autobiography of a Yogi*.

Swami Shankarananda guided the unfoldment of his devotees through established services at the Church, individual spiritual counseling, spiritual hypnotherapy, and the pure example of his own life.

He was a Kriya master and, as such, initiated devotees who were ready into the meditation practice of Kriya. A ten-disc CD set, *Kriya Yoga: Inner Path to God*, is available through Amazon.com.

He established the Universal Swami Order, based on the ancient Swami Order of India, and expanded it to include women and those who are married as well as unmarried. He was frequently called upon to speak at colleges and other organizations and at spiritual gatherings. He drew upon all the great scriptures and spiritual giants of the world to show the universality of truth at the mystical level and share his main message to cultivate unconditional love for all and to live the truths that have been given to humankind.

About the Editor

 Appointed by Swami Shankarananda as his successor, **Sri Swami Nityananda** carries on the spiritual lineage and teachings of universality and oneness at Divine Life Church, following joyfully in the path blazed by Swami Shankarananda. Her meditation talks focus on yoga philosophy and the practical application of yoga principles in daily life. She is known for her sense of humor, and for making ancient spiritual principles fresh and accessible to all. She welcomes people from every background, tradition, and way of life.

Swami Shankarananda consecrated her as a Swami and authorized her to conduct spiritual counseling and to initiate meditation students into Kriya yoga. He also appointed her as the minister and spiritual leader of Divine Life Church, where she now serves.

Swami Nityananda edited *The Yoga of the Lord's Prayer*. Swami Shankarananda then read through the edited book, yielding the current authorized edition. Swami Shankarananda also appointed Swami Nityananda to give talks and help spread the word about his beautiful teachings in *The Yoga of the Lord's Prayer*.

FOR MORE INFORMATION, PLEASE CONTACT

DARSHAN

Divine Life Church
5928 Falls Road
Baltimore, MD 21209
e-mail: divinelifestore@gmail.com
phone: 410-435-6121

Swami Shankarananda's books and CDs
are available through our online store at
www.DivineLifeChurch.org

and on Amazon at
amazon.com/author/swamishankaranandagiri

Made in the USA
Columbia, SC
10 April 2018